D1038161

SPECIAL EDUCATION
A Curriculum Guide

SPECIAL EDUCATION

A Curriculum Guide

Compiled and Edited by

EDWARD S. STARK, Ph.D.

Assistant Professor
Center for Special Education
Hofstra University
Hempstead, New York

With a Foreword by

Leon Charney, Ph.D.

Director
Center for Special Education
Hofstra University
Hempstead, New York

CHARLES C THOMAS • PUBLISHER
Springfield • Illinois • U.S.A.

Published and Distributed Throughout the World by
CHARLES C THOMAS • PUBLISHER

BANNERSTONE HOUSE
301-327 East Lawrence Avenue, Springfield, Illinois, U.S.A.

NATCHEZ PLANTATION HOUSE
735 North Atlantic Boulevard, Fort Lauderdale, Florida, U.S.A

© *1969, by* CHARLES C THOMAS • PUBLISHER

Library of Congress Catalog Card Number: 69-12067

With THOMAS BOOKS *careful attention is given to all details of
manufacturing and design. It is the Publisher's desire to present books
that are satisfactory as to their physical qualities and artistic possibilities
and appropriate for their particular use.* THOMAS BOOKS *will be true
to those laws of quality that assure a good name and good will.*

Printed in the United States of America
Q-1

Contributors

LEON CHARNEY, Ph.D.

Director
Center for Special Education
Hofstra University
Hempstead, New York

SAM LAMAGNA, M.A.

Principal, A.H.R.C. School
(School for the Association for the Help of Retarded Children)
Brookville, New York

EVELYN FARRELL, M.S.

Teacher for the Mentally Retarded
Massapequa, New York

LEON BARSKY, M.A.

Department of Special Education
Farmingdale Public Schools
Farmingdale, New York

ADELE HORN PAYERLE, M.S.

Teacher for the Mentally Retarded
Berner Senior High School
Massapequa, New York

ARTHUR HECHT, M.S.

Director of Pupil Personnel Services
Roosevelt Public Schools
Roosevelt, New York

MILTON LEVINE, M.S.

Director, A.H.R.C. Workshop
(Association for the Help of Retarded Children Workshop)
Hempstead, New York

v

ELEANOR ZOUEFF, M.S.

Teacher for the Brain Injured
Massapequa Public Schools
Massapequa, New York

PHILOMENA SINAGRA, M.A.

Teacher for the Brain Injured
McKenna Junior High School
Massapequa, New York

EMIL LOMBARDI, M.S.

Principal
Cerebral Palsy School
Roosevelt, New York

To two very "special" children
Alan and Helene

Foreword

THE growing awareness that the problems of intellectual, emotional, and physical deviation confront our nation with a major educational challenge has resulted in the publication of numerous texts of a survey nature. These survey texts play a vital role in orienting the reader to the field of special education and in presenting an overview of the characteristics of a wide range of exceptionality.

Less readily available are texts which attempt to familiarize the reader with the essential features of curriculum patterns currently implemented in school programs designed to meet the needs of children with intellectual, emotional, and physical disabilities. While numerous curriculum guides are available in the various areas of exceptionality, rarely have these been assembled in a single text.

The present volume has assembled under a single cover, curriculum guides in the areas of mental retardation, brain injury, and severe physical disability. Curriculum patterns within these areas are further subdivided on the basis of the needs of children at various age levels. Inasmuch as the material thus presented was drawn largely from the special education programs of a single school district, the material is characterized by a cohesive quality which could not be attained through perusal of randomly selected curriculum guides.

It is anticipated that those concerned with the implementation of effective educational programs for the deviant will find this volume of practical value as a guide to their endeavors.

LEON CHARNEY

Preface

THIS book received its birthday when the editor was Director of Special Education for the Massapequa, New York Public Schools. It had been painfully apparent for too long a time that much of the classroom teaching for the special children, while intelligently conceived, was too often rather haphazardly presented. The gap between design of curriculum and its execution was at times minor, at other times merely self-evident. But, too often, this gap was glaring. The end result was an inadequacy of communication between teacher and pupil, an ineffectiveness of liaison between teacher and administrator, and poor public relations between parents and the schools.

How many times parents wanted to know, What is the child learning? or Is there an outline of the course work I can look at? Inevitably, the school personnel were placed in an embarrassing position. Most embarrassed of all was the Director of Special Education, because unfortunately no such guide existed.

The scope, plan, and purpose of this book therefore was to create a concrete and comprehensive guide and course of study which, while originating from a desire to solidify our own Special Education Department, quickly became a much sought after instrument by surrounding school districts. It was apparent that we had hit upon a serious omission in the educational planning of most special education departments.

As our original plan developed, we enlarged upon it, always with one purpose in mind: Could the teacher in outlying rural districts as well as those in large cities utilize our curriculum guide in extending or initiating a special program in their own school district? The one-room schoolhouse or the fifteen school district shared a common problem—unifying and consolidating the teacher techniques for children in special classes as presented by master teachers. Our format was simple, yet highly effective. We would, where possible, create a triad of units, activities, and materials in the presentation of the curricula.

In order to most effectively present the program for the retarded, it was essential to include a chapter dealing with the trainable child. The educable child was well represented by chapters ranging from pre-primary to senior high school level (Work Study Program). However, because too little had been written on effective follow up with these children after high school graduation, we turned to an authority in the Sheltered Workshop Program to complete the treatment on the area of the retarded. The brain-injury classes both at the elementary and secondary levels were also included in this treatise on Special Education. Finally, it became apparent that unless we discussed the multiply physically handicapped child, our treatment of the subject would not be complete. Accordingly, a chapter on the crippled is included.

Although not a chapter by itself, the Editor's Comments are an attempt to round out the curriculum by including within the framework of this book services usually provided normal children, which he felt are too often denied children in special education.

Again, our purpose is to reach teachers everywhere who may have questions relating to the teaching of the special child. If we can meet their needs as professionals in the field and can assist in improving their class presentation, the purposes of this book will have been fulfilled and our professional obligation discharged.

EDWARD S. STARK

Contents

Part I
The Mentally Retarded

Part II
The Brain-Injured

Part III
The Severely Physically Handicapped

Part IV
Conclusion

SPECIAL EDUCATION
A Curriculum Guide

PART I
The Mentally Retarded

Chapter 1

The Trainable Mentally Retarded— A Philosophy

Sam A. La Magna

IN public education the trainable mental retardate is oftentimes defined in terms of intellect only. An individual whose intelligence quotient is 50 or below, as determined by an individually administered test of mental development by a certified psychologist or school psychologist, is considered to be only trainable. Furthermore, criteria imposed on public schools for the establishment of classes for the mentally retarded include only the nature of the child to be placed as determined by range of intellect (50 or below—trainable mental retardation; 50 to 75 —educable mental retardation), chronological age span of the class (a four-year age span is usually acceptable), and the number of youngsters who may be placed into one class. As guidelines for the establishment of special classes for the trainable mentally retarded, the existing criteria leaves much to be desired.

In practice, special educators have found that the trainable population is realistically one whose measurable intellect will range from approximately the mid 20's through the mid 60's. This is a population wherein some manifestation of organicity may be anticipated as a rule.[1] Educational achievement regarding academic skills is minimal. Functional academics, however, are stressed since this an area that will help the trainable to better understand and cope with his environment. In terms of educa-

---

[1] Report of the Task Force on Education and Rehabilitation—President's Panel on Mental Retardation, August 1962.

tional achievement, one will usually find that level of measurable intellect is highly correlated with level of conceptual abilities. The intelligence quotient, therefore, becomes a more significant means of predicting the educational potential within this population. In terms of educational differential diagnosis, this becomes very meaningful considering that in the area of "the brain-injured child," for instance, where one may anticipate a depressed level of functioning as well as a depressed level of intellect, one will also anticipate an obvious variability with either or both of these measures. This quantitative performance variability is not nearly as significant a characteristic of the trainable population.

The trainable mental retardate is one who demonstrates marked disabilities in all areas of adaptive behavior. Social behavioral characteristics are generally immature. Without the required supervision and structure in relation to social activities, the trainable's pattern will reflect very limited awareness or judgment of a situation. As a result, inappropriate socio-behavioral characteristics may be anticipated. The ability to communicate verbally is usually influenced by generally limited language development, physiological disabilities that may impede language as well as a marked immaturity concerning the overall comunications process.

Motor proficiency is generally depressed in both gross as well as refined areas. One ay anticipate an awkward gait, difficulty in running, hopping, skipping, and jumping as well as difficulties in terms of walking heel to toe in a prescribed manner or exercises involving the coordination of arm and leg movements. This population will demonstrate impaired functioning in terms of the ability to grasp as well as finger dexterity, which, in turn, will negatively influence abilities of a practical nature such as the manipulation of a crayon, pencil, and scissors. The Lincoln-Oseret-

---

² Sloan, W.: The Lincoln-Oseretsky Motor Development Scale. *Genetic Psychology Monographs*, 51:183-25, 1955.

³ Sloan, W.: Motor proficiency and intelligence, *American Journal of Mental Deficiency*, 55:394-406, 1951.

⁴ Rabin, H. M.: The Relationship of Age, Intelligence, and Sex to Motor Deficiency in Mental Defectives, *American Journal of Mental Deficiency*, 62:507-516, 1957.

sky Motor Performance Scale[2] has been utilized by researchers to discern comparative motor performance abilities between various disability groups. Sloan[3] and Rabin[4] attempted to discern the relationship of age, sex, and intelligence to motor proficiency, utilizing the Lincoln-Oseretsky scale. Sloan found that children of normal intellect performed significantly better than the mentally retarded. Rabin, in a study confined to mental retardates with no suggestion of brain damage, found a significant relationship in terms of age only.

Heath[5] in a study concerned with brain-injured and endogenous mental retardates demonstrated that the endogenous group performed significantly better than the brain-injured mental retardate.

The above mentioned areas include some of the characteristics which may further serve the educator to distinguish between that individual who is truly trainable from the many other areas of exceptionality which we encounter. It should be realized, however, that the trainable population should not be approached by the educator as a global population with entirely comparable patterns of behavior or performance. Although we are dealing with a limited range of performance expectancy, there are certainly differences within it which should be reflected in terms of the educational program.

Considering the many areas wherein this population is deviant from the norm, the organization of classes for these youngsters would certainly reflect more feasible criteria. A four year age range, regarding class organization, for instance, must bring together youngsters at various levels of readiness in all spheres of behavior. This readily accepted practice must, by its nature, present the teacher as well as the class group with an immediate structural problem. Within a normal population, we may anticipate commonalities of performance in relation to the maturational process. Therefore, levels of abilities concerning performance areas such as motor proficiency, language, and conceptual development would be very similar for all six-, seven-, or eight-year-

---

[5] Heath, S.: Railwalking Performance as Related to Mental Age and Etiological Types, *American Journal of Psychology*, 55:240-247, 1942.

olds, etc. At the same time, in public education, we still realize it is necessary to maintain a very close chronological age range for each of the grades from kindergarten through twelfth grade since, although there are basic commonalities among the various youngsters of any single age, we must still anticipate differences of a more subtle nature which may influence a youngster's performance abiilty. These differences may be a result of factors such as personality, modes of behavior, motivational needs, differences in life experiences, adn differences in the ability to assimilate new information.

The necessity of an intelligent and feasible approach to the grouping of youngsters is much more necessary within a trainable population, considering that the basic maturational commonalities are not nearly as uniform as they are among a normal population. We, therefore, must anticipate differences within a single age grouping and establish criteria of a qualitative nature for the placement of youngsters of the same age group within various classes. The various classes then will reflect the needs of the children by virtue of the nature of the various class programs.

Although the concept and philosophy concerning the education of the trainable mentally retarded child indicates the realistic expectation that they will not be independent within the community at large, the training program for these youngsters should be geared, however, to inculcate a desire to provide the necessary experiential opportunities to enable these youngsters to achieve as independent a level of functioning as possible within a framework of their recognized limitations. Educationally this can be achieved through a centralized facility for the trainable mentally retarded, since the term education infers much more than the more familiar concepts of formalized programing.

A centralized school structure for these youngsters is admittedly unique in terms of public education. However, many educators involved with these youngsters are becoming more and more convinced that realistic adjustments within the educational process must be made and that these adjustments will provide us with the only feasible answer to the many problems of educating the trainable mentally retarded individual. Deficiencies in all areas of adaptive behavior, we realize, are characteristic of this population. For this reason, we should not attempt to subject individuals within this population to community settings or structures, including those concerned with education which are geared to the norm of our society. By centralizing classes for the trainable, we can achieve a number of basic objectives of sound education which, in turn, would have significant meaning to the trainable mentally retarded. These basic objectives will include the following:

1. **Homogeneity**

    The greater the number of students within the educational facility, the greater the opportunity of area groupings of like students within the setting and the greater the opportunity of increased homogeneity within each classroom. Considering the limited incidence of individuals within this educational classification, we must realize that in any one school district or community the number of trainable youth of school age will be limited. If attempts at establishing classes are made on an individualized community or district basis, the likelihood of establishing a single class with a very wide age range must be expected. Through cooperative efforts of communities or school districts, one will find the necessary numbers of students to group classes so that the chronological range is feasible as well as allowing one to group youngsters with like performance abilities.

2. **Social Factors**

    Through centralization it is possible to develop a culture in which the youngster may have every opportunity to be exposed to and, therefore, relate to a true peer group. Trainable youngsters placed within an elementary or secondary school setting are not provided with this opportunity where the social relationships are limited only to those youngsters within their one class grouping. If we relate back and consider that this one class grouping accounts for youngsters with a wide age range as well as performance ability range, one realizes that the problem is even more significant than it appears to be. A social relationship is very much dependent on one's acceptance as a true peer by others. It was indicated earlier that the normal child's social relationship with the trainable is not on this level and cannot be expected to be, just as one cannot expect a trainable youngster to maintain himself in a social relationship with normal children.

Within a centralized facility, however, the opportunities for interpersonal relationships of true peers is greatly increased. It is only within such a situation that a trainable individual will learn to socially relate in an appropriate manner, which is certainly a prerequisite to his appropriate social behavior in other settings.

3. **Understanding One's Environment**

The ability to become familiar with one's environment through true interaction and experience is imperative. A centralized school facility allows the youngster much more latitude and mobility since wherever he goes within the facility, he will find it possible to relate to the other students, any adults, and whatever else he may see or hear, since the facility's orientation is directed towards this end.

4. **Ancillary Services**

In a centralized facility the teacher enjoys the opportunity of having the necessary supportive ancillary services available such as the school psychologist, social worker, speech teacher, nurse, physical education teacher, music teacher, and dental hygienist. Grouping of appropriate personnel should not be overlooked as a most significant factor in the education of the trainable mentally retarded. This multi-discipline approach which is feasible within a centralized facility will provide one with the means of intensified evaluations, remedial programing, and communications with home as well as other community agencies. The special class for the trainable, situated in an isolated setting within the elementary or secondary school, will not enjoy nearly the extent of supportive intensified services which may be made available through centralization.

5. **Structure**

The global program for the trainable mentally retarded

should be developmental and goal-oriented in nature. For this reason, the instructional program as well as the environmental routines and physical setting should be devised to enhance one's ability to adapt appropriately to the specific objectives as well as the general goals of a particular level of programing. This necessary aspect of controlling the environmental setting may be readily achieved through centralization of programing for the trainable mentally retarded.

The following is the Curriculum Outline Guide of the program at the Nassau County Special Services School For the Mentally Retarded:

I. Social Studies Skills
   A. Self-Awareness Concept Training
   B. Self-Help—Eating
   C. Self-Help—Dressing
   D. Self-Help—Personal Hygiene
   E. Occupational Social Skills for Daily Living
   F. The Family
   G. The Home
   H. The Community
   I. Citizenship
   J. Transportation
   K. Holidays

II. Health Skills
   A. Physical Hygiene
   B. Clothing
   C. Proper Foods
   D. Health Habit Training (Preventative)
   E. Mental Health Skills (For leisure time recreation)

III. Language Arts Skills
   A. Communication Skills—Verbal
   B. Communication Skills—Auditory
   C. Word Recognition
   D. Reading Readiness
   E. Functional Reading
   F. Writing Readiness
   G. Writing

IV. Mathematics Sequence
  A. Discriminatory Concepts
  B. Number Concepts
  C. Arithmetic Sequence
  D. Time
  E. Money

V. Science
  A. Origin of Foods
  B. Plant Life
  C. Animal Life
  D. Signs of the Seasons of the Year
  E. Weather
  F. Our Planet
  G. Sky Solar Bodies

VI. Sensory Concept Training
  A. Visual
  B. Auditory
  C. Tactile
  D. Gustatory
  E. Olfactory

VII. Safety Habit Training
  A. The Home
  B. The Community
  C. The School
  D. The Bus

VIII. Arts and Crafts
  A. Personal Development
  B. Occupational Skills Development
  C. Gross Motor Control
  D. Fine Motor Control

IX. Physical Education
  A. Competitive Games
  B. Calisthenics
  C. Activities for Healthy Physical Development
  D. Gross Motor Skills
  E. Fine Motor Skills

X. Cultural Appreciation
  A. Music

B. Art
C. Dancing
D. Literature

The following are the developmental aims and objectives as related to the activity areas described in the curriculum outline.

PRIMARY AIMS AND OBJECTIVES

I. Social Studies Skills

A. Self-Awareness Concept Training
  To become consciously aware of oneself through the ability.
  1. To learn to answer to one's name.
  2. To learn to know whether one is a boy or a girl.
  3. To learn to identify oneself in a mirror.
  4. To learn to identify oneself in a picture.
  5. To learn to identify the parts of one's body.
  6. To learn to express one's name.
  7. To learn to identify one's printed name.
  8. To learn to recognize one's age.

B. Self-Help—Eating
  1. To learn to wash hands before meals.
  2. To learn acceptable and courteous table manners.
  3. To learn to use a napkin without being reminded.
  4. To learn to eat what is served.
  5. To learn to develop the ability to eat solid foods with the appropriate utensils.
  6. To learn to drink from a cup or glass.
  7. To learn the use of a straw for drinking.
  8. To learn to pour liquids.
  9. To learn proper eating habits.
  10. To learn to begin eating only after everyone has been served.
  11. To learn to stay at the table until others have finished eating.

C. Self-Help—Dressing
  1. To learn to recognize one's own clothing.
  2. To learn to put on and remove clothing with minimum assistance.
    a. To learn to button and unbotton one's clothing.
    b. To learn the use of a zipper.
    c. To learn to put on and remove overshoes.
    d. To learn to tie and untie shoe laces.

3. To learn to put one's clothing in the proper place.
4. To learn to hang outer garments on a clothing hanger.
5. To learn to choose appropriate clothing for the occasion.
6. To learn to recognize suitable clothing for the weather.

D. Self-Help—Personal Hygiene
   1. To learn to wash and dry hands and face.
   2. To learn the proper method of brushing teeth.
   3. To learn to comb and brush hair.
   4. To learn the significance and technique of cleaning nails.
   5. To learn the importance of bathing regularly.
   6. To learn the importance of maintaining a neat appearance.
   7. To learn the importance of toilet habits.
      a. To learn to anticipate the need of going to the toilet and making the need known.
      b. To learn to flush after toileting.
      c. To learn to wash hands thoroughly after toileting.
      d. To learn to manage outer clothing before and after toileting.
      e. To learn to maintain a regular schedule of toileting daily.

E. Occupational Social Skills for Daily Living
   To prepare the child to his utmost capacity for living in a group, family situation, and for working with others in an economic situation, cooperatively and with interest, understanding, minimal instruction, and appropriate behavior, by developing a responsible attitude toward himself and others, while alone or with his group, at leisure time or while participating in work activities.
   1. To develop an understanding and meaning of:
      a. rights and feelings of others
      b. cooperation with peers and adults
      c. friendship
   2. To learn to ask for help when needed.
   3. To learn to play and work with others cooperatively
   4. To learn to share possessions.
   5. To learn to share common property.
   6. To learn to respect the property rights of others.
   7. To learn the meaning of responsibility.
      a. in the care of personal articles such as:
         (1) comb and brush
         (2) toothbrush
         (3) lunchbox
         (4) handkerchief

       b. in the care of materials issued in class.

       c. in learning to replace materials in the appropriate place after use.

   8. To learn cooperation.

       a. To learn to help others when others seek help.

       b. To learn to help willingly with tasks at school and at home.

   9. To learn dependability.

       a. To learn to carry notes from school to home and from home to school.

       b. To learn to carry out errands within the school.

  10. To learn perseverance.

       a. To learn to keep working at an assigned task until completed or until one is instructed to stop.

       b. To learn to develop an attitude of willingness by attempting a task after an unsuccessful try.

  11. To learn honesty and truthfulness.

       a. To learn to develop a respect for authority or persons in authority.

       b. To learn to understand and acknowledge the fact when one does something wrong.

       c. To learn to return or report found articles.

       d. To learn to develop a sense of fairness and honesty in work and play.

F. The Family

   1. To learn to recognize the members of one's immediate family (e.g. Mother is a woman, father is a man, etc.).

   2. To learn to become aware of the duties (roles) of each member of the family.

   3. To learn to become a more useful member of the family (e.g. through household tasks).

G. The Home

   1. To learn the different rooms in the house:

       a. their names

       b. their uses

   2. To learn the different types of furniture found in each room.

   3. To learn the importance of cleanliness in the home (e.g. the use of mops, brooms, etc.).

   4. To become aware of the different types of homes (e.g. apartment houses, etc.).

H. The Community

1. To become acquainted with one's immediate neighborhood.
2. To become aware of the make up of the neighborhood (stores, houses of worship, railroads, etc.).
3. To become aware of the community helpers (recognize by sight and name).
4. To become aware of the role of our community helpers (milkman, postman, baker, fireman, policeman, etc.).
5. To become aware of the community helpers who keep us healthy (doctors, nurses, dentist, etc.).

I. Citizenship

1. Citizenship training.
   a. To learn to recognize the American flag.
   b. To learn to practice the Pledge of Allegiance and sing the flag song.
   c. To learn that we live in the United States of America.
   d. To become aware that we are all Americans.
2. Geographic concepts.
   a. To learn to recognize where one lives.
   b. To learn that we live in different towns.
   c. To learn that we live in one larger community (e.g. Long Island).
3. Current events.
   a. To recognize famous people such as the President of the United States.
   b. To develop an interest in current events by watching television, listening to the radio, and looking at pictures.

J. Transportation

1. To learn the different modes of transportation.
   a. Land
      (1) bicycle
      (2) roller skates
      (3) wagons
      (4) car
      (5) bus
      (6) truck
      (7) train
   b. Water (boats, ships).
   c. Air
2. To learn the reasons for transportation (carrying foods, people, and other products).

K. Holidays
   1. To learn to associate holidays with the months.
   2. To learn to associate holidays with the seasons of the year.
   3. To learn the significance of our major holidays.
   4. To learn to develop a sense of our customs and our national history through holidays.

II. Health Skills

   A. Physical Hygiene
      1. To learn the importance of personal cleanliness.
      2. To recognize the needs of establishing the following practices:
         a. washing hands and face at appropriate times
         b. brushing teeth regularly
         c. bathing regularly
         d. keeping one's hair clean and neat at all times
      3. To learn to attend to personal needs on a regular basis each day.
      4. To recognize and practice good posture habits when standing, sitting, and walking.
      5. To learn the need of daily fresh air.
      6. To learn the importance of a full night's sleep.

   B. Clothing
      1. To learn the appropriate type of clothing for different kinds of weather.
      2. To learn that clothing protects the body.
      3. To learn that clean clothing is important to good health.

   C. Proper Foods
      1. To learn to develop good eating habits by eating slowly, chewing well, etc.
      2. To learn to recognize the foods that make up a well-balanced breakfast, lunch, and dinner.
      3. To learn the importance of eating three good meals a day.

   D. Health Habit Training (Preventative)
      1. To learn to carry a handkerchief or tissue and to use it correctly.
      2. To learn to wash hands after eating or toileting.
      3. To learn not to put foreign objects or fingers into one's mouth.

4. To learn not to touch a public drinking fountain with one's mouth.
5. To become aware of the following health danger signals and learn to report them to parent when at home, and the teacher when at school:
   a. chills
   b. sneezing
   c. coughing
   d. headaches
   e. stomach aches
   f. excessive fatigue
6. To learn to avoid close contact with people who are ill, who have colds, etc.
7. To learn the importance of taking medicines when sick.
8. To learn not to take medicine in the home, school, or any other place unless administered by the proper person (parent, nurse, etc.).

E. Mental Health Skills (For leisure time and recreation)
1. To derive self-satisfaction by playing alone, through the use of following media:
   a. crayons, paints
   b. clay
   c. puzzles
   d. books
2. To derive satisfaction through participating socially with others (playing group games, listening to stories, etc.).
3. To teach the child to become aware of and to follow rules and develop a sense of sportsmanship in winning and losing.

III. Language Arts Skills

A. Communication Skills—Verbal
1. To upgrade communication to one's optimal level through gesture or verbalization.
2. To learn to express one's self verbally when making requests.
3. To learn to identify persons, familiar objects, foods, etc. by name.
4. To learn to respond to a question verbally.
5. To learn to look at a picture and describe it verbally.
6. To learn to carry a simple verbal message.
7. To learn to relate a simple experience verbally.
8. To learn to tell a short story or describe a favorite toy verbally.

B. Communication Skills—Auditory
   1. To become aware of one's own voice.
   2. To learn to listen to others.
   3. To learn to respond to a verbal command.
   4. To learn to distinguish different sounds (voices, bells, sirens, clock, etc.).
   5. To learn to recognize the voices of those in one's class.

C. Word Recognition
   1. To learn to identify one's name, address, telephone number, and other names in the class.
   2. To learn to relate (associate) basic functional words to pictures (boys, girls, walk, run, tree, house).
   3. To learn to identify functional words independent of pictures (exit, poison, in, out, men's, ladies,' etc.).

D. Reading Readiness
   1. To learn to identify familiar colors (red, yellow, brown, etc.).
   2. To learn to identify and name geometric forms (square, circle, triangle).
   3. To learn the sequence of movement from the left (by following a moving pointer, by utilizing painting with the left to right movement, by utilizing a paint brush and making horizontal lines).
   4. To learn left to right orientation.
   5. To learn to recognize and name objects placed in a left to right sequence.
   6. To learn to identify similarites and differences in a picture.
   7. To learn to recognize things missing in a picture or a sequence of pictures.

E. Functional Reading (not at this level)

F. Writing Readiness
   1. To learn how to hold a pencil, crayon, and paintbrush properly.
   2. To learn to hold paper properly.
   3. To learn correct posture in writing, drawing, etc.
   4. To learn to trace over simple forms and shapes.
   5. To learn to trace over a line, number, or letter.
   6. To learn to trace over dotted lines.
   7. To learn the sequence of left to right when writing.

G. Writing
  1. To learn to copy simple letters, numbers, etc.
  2. To learn to write letters and numbers independently.
  3. To learn to write one's own name and home address.

IV. Mathematics Sequence

  A. Discriminatory Concepts
  To make the child aware of differences in terms of quantity and position
    1. Quantity:
      a. large—small
      b. big—little
      c. long—short
      d. wide—narrow, etc.
    2. Position:
      a. up—down
      b. high—low
      c. on—off
      d. left—right
      e. under—over
      f. beginning—end
      g. open—shut, etc.

  B. Number Concepts
    1. To learn one's telephone, street, and bus number.
    2. To learn to count (limits should be the highest number that the child understands the concept of).
    3. To make one aware that numbers tell "How Many."
    4. To learn to recognize the written number.

  C. Arithmetic Sequence
    1. To learn to sort and match objects according to color, size, and form.
    2. To learn the number of days in a week and months in a year.
    3. To learn the relationships of one number to another (2 is more than 1 and less than 3).

  D. Time
    1. To learn the names of the days of the week.
    2. To learn the names of the months in a year.
    3. To learn the names of the seasons of the year.

4. To learn the differences between daytime, nighttime, morning, afternoon, today, tomorrow, yesterday.
5. To learn to associate various daily events with the time of day.
6. To learn there are two hands on a clock, a large hand and a small hand.
7. To learn to recognize the numbers on a clock and associate them with the time of day.
8. To learn that the small hand points to the hour of the day.
9. To learn to associate the hour of the day by the direction of the small hand.

E. Money
   1. To learn that we can buy things with money. (*Note*: It is imperative that real money be used during any activity in this area.)
   2. Learn to identify and name a penny, nickel, dime, quarter, and half-dollar.
   1. To learn to recognize and name various bills by the number printed in each corner of the bill.

V. Science

A. Origins of foods
   1. To learn that some foods come from plant life.
   2. To learn that some foods come from animal life.
   3. To learn that some of our food is found in water.
   4. To learn that some foods come from near our home and others come from far away.

B. Plant Life
   1. To learn that plants are living things.
   2. To learn what a plant needs to grow healthy (soil, water. sunlight, and plant food).
   3. To learn how a plant grows (from seed, bulb, transplanting, etc.).
   4. To learn that some plants are edible and others are not edible.
   5. To learn the different parts of a plant (roots, stems, leaves. etc.).
   6. To learn the names of various plants.

C. Animal Life
   1. To learn to recognize and name familiar animals (dogs, cats, birds, cows, horses, sheep, deer, etc.).
   2. To learn what different animals eat to stay healthy.
   3. To learn that animals are different in many ways (colors. shapes, body coverings).
   4. To learn how animals are useful to man:
      a. food
      b. clothing
      c. help in work
      d. pets
   5. To learn how to care for pets.

D. Signs of the Seasons of the Year
   To learn the different characteristics of each of the four seasons.
   1. Temperature
   2. Precipitation (rain, snow, sleet, hail)
   3. Length of the day (greater in summer, less in winter)

E. Weather
   1. To learn that there are different elements of weather (sun, clouds, rain, wind, snow, temperature, etc.).
   2. To observe and feel changes in weather (weather can change within a given day).
   3. To learn that temperature is measured by a thermometer.
   4. To learn that there are variations in temperature (hot, warm, cool, cold, etc.).
   5. To learn that weather can effect one's activities.
   6. To learn how weather can effect plants and animals.

F. Our Planet
   1. To learn that the world in which we live is called the Earth.
   2. To learn that the Earth consists of land, water, and air.

G. Sky Solar Bodies
   1. To learn that we can see the sun every day.
   5. To learn the colors and shape of the sun.
   3. To learn that we can see the moon every night.
   4. To learn that we can see stars at night.

VI. Sensory Concept Training

A. Visual
  1. To learn to identify familiar objects (colors, figures, etc.).
  2. To learn to visually discriminate between familiar objects.
  3. To learn to visually associate familiar objects with colors, shapes, sizes, figures.
  4. To learn to identify specific shapes and sizes (e.g. as found in signs).
  5. To learn to visually discriminate between specific shapes and sizes.
  6. To learn to visually associate specific shapes and sizes to objects.

B. Auditory
  1. To learn to identify familiar sounds (bell, horn, siren, etc.).
  2. To learn to discriminate between different familiar sounds.
  3. To learn to associate familiar sounds to objects.
  4. To learn to reproduce various sounds.

C. Tactile
  1. To learn to identify some familiar objects.
  2. To learn to discriminate between familiar objects.
  3. To learn to associate familiar objects by using the tactile sensations.
  4. To learn to identify the tactile sensations of:
     a. hot—cold
     b. hard—soft
     c. wet—dry
     d. sharp—dull
  5. To learn to discriminate between these tactile sensations.
  6. To learn to associate tactile sensations to objects.
  7. To learn to identify different textures of materials.
  8. To learn to discriminate between different textures of materials.
  9. To learn to associate different textures to different materials.

D. Gustatory
  1. To learn to identify the tastes of familiar foods.
  2. To learn to discriminate different tastes of foods.
  3. To learn to associate tastes to foods.

E. Olfactory
  1. To learn to identify familiar odors (soap, paint, etc.).
  2. To learn to discriminate between different odors.

3. To learn to associate odors to objects.
4. To learn to identify odors of familiar foods.
5. To learn to discriminate between odors of familiar foods.
6. To learn to associate different odors to different foods.

VII. Safety Habit Training

To make the child aware of the potential dangers in and around the home, school, and community, and to teach the child some practical safety habits.

A. The Home
1. To teach the child not to run through the house except in designated play areas.
2. To teach the child to avoid running on stairs.
3. To teach the child not to climb on chairs, tables, stoves, sinks, desks, etc.
4. To learn to put away toys, tools, clothes, etc. in their proper places to prevent accidents.
5. To teach the child not to play with matches.
6. To teach the child not to touch, handle, or play with stoves.
7. To teach the child not to handle, touch, or play with electric outlets or tools.

B. The Community
1. To teach the child safety on the streets:
   a. cross at corners
   b. cross at the green light
   c. stop at the red light
   d. look both ways before crossing
   e. walk on the sidewalk
   f. watch policeman's signal
2. To learn how and where to use wagons, bicycles, scooters, etc.
3. To learn how and where to use skates.
4. To teach the children not to accept walks, rides, treats, etc. from strangers.
5. To learn to keep away from lots, buildings, garages, and basements that are under construction or unoccupied.

C. The School
1. To learn the proper procedures when passing through the halls of a school building:

a. no running, pushing, or shoving
b. staying in line, keeping to right
c. holding partner's hand
2. To learn to avoid accidents in the classroom by:
    a. walking, not pushing or fighting
    b. not climbing on chairs, tables, etc.
    c. remembering to put away toys, tools, and materials
    d. learning how to properly use scissors, rulers, needles, pencils, etc.
3. To learn and perform proper fire drill procedures.
4. To be able to achieve the specified playground rules and behavior:
    a. no fighting or pushing
    b. staying with class (no wandering)
    c. using equipment properly
    d. waiting in line for your turn
    e. learning not to climb on the school yard fence

D. The Bus
    1. To learn to wait for the bus in an orderly manner (quietly, in line, no fighting or pushing).
    2. To learn to enter a bus properly:
        a. wait at the designated spot until bus comes to a stop
        b. hold onto railing or driver when entering bus
        c. take one's seat immediately
    3. To learn the correct behavior on a bus:
        a. stay seated with hands and feet in proper place
        b. talk quietly
        c. not to disturb or annoy the bus driver
        d. not to disturb or annoy other passengers
        e. keep hands, head, objects inside the window
        f. keep objects in their proper places
        g. to learn to leave a bus in an orderly fashion
        h. wait till the bus stops
        i. not to push or run when leaving bus
        j. hold onto guide rails

VIII. Arts and Crafts

A. Personal Development
    1. To develop and encourage growth and individuality through arts and crafts.
    2. To broaden one's leisure time through the use of arts and crafts.

    3. To acquire a sense of security by expressing oneself through arts and crafts.

    4. To acquire pleasure in the doing and making of products.

    5. To derive pleasure from making and giving things to others (cards, presents, wrapping paper, etc.).

B. Occupational Skills Development

    1. To learn to listen and follow instructions.

    2. To become familiar with the different types of media (crayons, finger paints, tempera, water colors, chalks, leather, straw, loops, wood, metal, clay, papers, etc.).

    3. To become familiar with the different types of tools used in arts and crafts (hammers, punches, scissors, looms, needles, sandpaper, staple machines etc.).

    4. To learn to identify tools and media.

    5. To develop skills in handling and using tools and media.

    6. To learn to care for and store tools and media.

C. Gross Motor Control

    1. To learn to use the large muscles.

    2. To learn to control the large muscles.

    3. To learn to develop arm-hand coordination.

D. Fine Motor Control

    1. To develop eye, hand, and finger coordination.

    2. To strengthen finger-hand coordination.

    3. To develop the ability to hold and use tools and media (pencils, crayons, paint brushes, scissors, needles, looms, laces, straw, etc.).

IX. Physical Education

A. Competitive Games

    1. To acquire the ability to cooperate with others and to learn to take part in organized play.

    2. To develop a spirit of competition.

    3. To develop skills necessary to be able to compete with individuals or teams.

    4. To motivate one to use more effort.

    5. To provide the child with more vigorous exercises.

    6. To acquire a sense of security through the use of skills used in competitive games.

    7. To stimulate and increase mental awareness.

    8. To relieve tensions.

B. Calisthenics
1. To learn the need for daily exercise.
2. To develop better growth of one's body through exercises.
3. To acquire better muscular development and control.
4. To develop endurance by increasing one's stamina and breath control.
5. To develop strength in one's body.
6. To develop grace and balance of one's movements.
7. To develop a sense of relaxation and relief of one's tensions.

C. Activities for Healthy Physical Development
1. Mat activities
   a. To learn to limber and flex one's body.
   b. To learn to protect oneself when falling.
   c. To develop a sense of timing.
   d. To develop a sense of rhythm.
2. Rope Exercises
   a. To develop arm and leg muscles.
   b. To develop a sense of coordination and body control.
   c. To develop a sense of timing.

D. Gross Motor Skills
Development and coordination of body
1. Whole body movement.
2. Leg-foot movement.
3. Arm-hand movement.
4. To overcome awkward and clumsy movements.
5. To develop muscular strength and control of large muscles.

E. Fine Motor Skills
1. To develop hand-finger coordination.
2. To develop eye-hand-finger coordination.
3. To improve the strength of one's eyes, hands, and fingers.

X. Cultural Appreciation

To make one aware of different forms of art.
A. Music
1. To develop an understanding of music.
   a. To acquire a knowledge of different types of music (marching, dancing, singing, listening, games, etc.).
   b. To develop an awareness of different kinds of rhythm (e.g. slow, fast, high, low, etc.).

    c. To develop a knowledge of various common instruments (horns, pianos, drums, etc.).

  2. To be able to enjoy music by:

    a. listening for pleasure

    b. listening for relaxation

    c. participating in musical activities (e.g. songs, dances, games, etc.)

  3. To learn movement and expression through music and musical activities.

  4. To improve one's speech through use of music (e.g. songs, choral speaking, etc.).

  5. To learn to discriminate between different kinds of music.

  6. To learn that music can produce different feelings and can be used at different times.

B. Art

  1. To learn to understand art.

    a. To learn the different medias used.

    b. To learn to develop a feeling for art forms and shapes.

    c. To learn to know the basic colors.

  2. To create a feeling of pleasure from art.

    a. Finding enjoyment in seeing art forms (commercial or child-made).

    b. The creation of different art forms through:

      (1) tracing

      (2) copying

      (3) coloring

      (4) free form, etc.

  3. To learn to develop certain skills in order to create art (e.g. coloring, shaping, grouping, etc.).

  4. To learn to differentiate different colors, shapes, forms.

C. Dancing

  1. To learn to recognize different dances (square, interpretative ballet, etc.).

  2. To learn to acquire a pleasure from watching dancing.

  3. To become aware of the pleasure of moving one's body to music by:

    a. learning tempos

    b. learning rhythms

    c. participation in dancing and dance exercises

  4. To help one to improve their grace and coordination.

D. Literature (not at this level)

INTERMEDIATE AIMS AND OBJECTIVES

I. Social Studies

  A. Self-Awareness Concept Training
   1. To learn to identify the parts of the body (arms, hands, eyes, nose, etc.).
   2. To learn to recognize parts of the body.
   3. To learn to name the parts of the body.
   4. To know the uses of the parts of the body.
   5. To learn to distinguish between the two genders (c.f. other children in class).
   6. To become aware of the names that go with the two genders (boy, girl, Mr., Miss, Mrs., female, male, etc.).
   7. To learn to relate to words such as I, me, mine, you, yours, his, hers, etc.
   8. To learn that one is a whole person and to learn how to act as a whole person.
   9. To learn to acquire a sense of security and accomplishment by being able to do a job by oneself and make use of one's abilities.

  B. Self-Help
   1. To learn to become a more independent individual by being able to complete certain tasks by oneself (e.g. tying shoes, dressing, eating correctly, etc.).
   2. To develop good habits and to learn to abolish bad ones.

  C. Occupational Social Skills for Daily Living
   1. To develop the ability to accept criticism as well as praise.
   2. To learn to assume the responsibility of finishing an assigned task.
   3. To learn to work independently on assigned tasks.
   4. To learn to control one's temper.
   5. To learn the importance of keeping one's word.
   6. To learn not to use exaggerations.
   7. To learn to use acceptable language at all times.
   8. To learn to establish worthwhile work habits and responsibilities.
   9. To learn to become aware of "appropriate" relationships between people (brother-sister; husband-wife).
   10. To learn one's address and telephone number.

D. The Family

1. To learn to identify all the members of one's immediate family.
2. To develop a sense of cooperation and importance of one's immediate family.
3. To learn to live happily in a family setting.
4. To learn to recognize and understand the differences between the immediate family and other relatives such as aunts, uncles, cousins, and grandparents.
5. To develop an understanding of one's relationships to other relatives.

E. The Home

1. To learn the different materials that go into making a home (e.g. wood, bricks, tile, cement).
2. To learn how a home obtains heat, light, and water.
3. To learn that the home is the center of a family group.
4. To learn to have a sense of pride in one's home.
5. To learn how to become a more useful member of one's home.
   a. Keeping one's room neat and clean.
   b. Learning how to use the phone in one's house.
   c. Being able to care for one's garden.
   d. Learning how to use and care for household tools.

F. The Community

1. To learn the name of one's village, town, or city.
2. To learn that each person lives in a village, town, or city which may differ from one's own village, town, or city.
3. To learn to know the larger community in which one lives (outside of the immediate neighborhood).
4. To learn the make up of the larger community (buses, trucks, department stores, amusement centers, shopping centers, etc.).
5. To learn to become aware of the buildings of the larger community (e.g. firehouses, schools, police stations, hospitals, homes, and workshops.).
6. To learn the purposes of these buildings and the people associated with them (e.g. firehouse-fireman; hospital-doctor and/or nurse.).
7. To introduce the concept of community living and how people work and live together.

G. Citizenship
  1. To develop citizenship training.
      a. To become aware of certain national symbols:
          (1) eagle
          (2) colors
          (3) motto
      b. To become aware of certain state symbols:
          (1) flag
          (2) colors
          (3) flowers
  2. To develop geographic concepts.
      a. To learn that we live in New York State and that New York State is part of the United States of America.
      b. To learn that there are other states which together make up the United States of America.
      c. To learn that there are other countries besides the United States of America.
      d. To learn that the world is round.
      e. To learn that these other countries are made up of people who have different customs, languages, etc.
      f. To learn that we get food and products from these other countries.
  3. To learn about current events:
      a. To become aware of daily current events.
      b. To learn that current events can effect one's life or one's family.

H. Transportation
  1. To learn that transportation can and does change.
  2. To learn why transportation is necessary for daily life:
      a. car for father to go to work
      b. car for mother to go to store
      c. bus for children to go to school, work, etc.
      d. trucks to bring food which we need to grow
  3. To learn to recognize and identify parts of cars, boats, trucks, planes, etc. (such as motors, windshield wipers, doors, trunks, wings, sails, and windows)
  4. To understand how certain modes of transportation work (car uses motor, boat uses sails, plane needs wings).

I. Holidays
  1. To learn the meaning of and why we celebrate major holidays.

    2. To learn special words that are connected with holidays (pilgrims, veterans, jack-o'-lanterns, etc.).

II. Health Skills

  A. Physical Hygiene

    To become aware of certain practices that will enhance one's well-being.
    1. To learn to bathe regularly.
    2. To learn to brush teeth regularly.
    3. To learn to wash face and hands.
    4. To learn to comb one's hair.

  B. Clothing

    1. To learn to change wet or dirty clothing as soon as possible
    2. To recognize when clothing is not properly fitted (e.g. tight shoes, pants, skirts, shirts, etc.).
    3. To learn the significance of protective clothing and how it protects one (e.g. rubbers, rainhats, and raincoats, etc.).

  C. Proper Foods

    1. To learn such groups of foods as milk products, breads, etc., and to eat a variety of foods from each group.
    2. To learn not to overeat and to eat proper foods at snack time.
    3. To learn the importance of cleaning food before eating it.
    4. To learn that some foods must be cooked and others can be eaten raw.
    5. To learn that food can spoil.
    6. To learn how to recognize spoiled food (e.g. sour milk, moldy bread).
    7. To learn how different foods effect the body:
      a. milk—strong teeth
      b. meat—muscles
      c. fish and carrots—strong eyes

  D. Health Habit Training (Preventative)

    1. To develop some understanding of how disease is transmitted.
    2. To learn the importance of seeing a doctor and dentist regularly.
    3. To learn to report accidents and illnesses immediately.
    4. To learn not to pick sores, cuts, bruises, etc. in order not to cause infections.

E. Mental Health Skills (For leisure time and recreation)
   1. To recognize and set limits for oneself.
   2. To learn to make simple choices and find things to do by oneself.
   3. To encourage positive attitudes towards oneself as well as others in work or play.
   4. To learn to play indoors as well as outdoors in an individual or group situation.
   5. To learn how to develop a hobby.

III. Language Arts Skills

   A. Communication Skills—Verbal
   To be able to relate to others and to make individual wants known.
      1. To learn to express oneself in an understandable manner, and to learn to converse when communicating with others rather than by gestures.
      2. To learn to use a larger variety of words when describing objects.
      3. To learn to sing words to music.
      4. To learn to participate in dramatic plays.
      5. To learn to use polite terms of expression, (e.g. thank you, please, you're welcome).
      6. To learn to converse by using short sentences.
      7. To learn to use appropriate verbs rather than general terms to describe persons, places or things.

   B. Communication Skills—Auditory
      1. To learn to listen to stories, records, plays, etc.
      2. To learn to recognize the importance points of a story, play, or record, etc.
      3. To learn to listen to and recognize the sounds of musical instruments.

   C. Word Recognition
      1. To learn to recognize words through association with pictures, charts, etc.
      2. To learn to recognize words seen in one's environment.
      3. To learn to read simple sentences made up of functional words.

D. Reading Readiness
   1. To acquire a visual perception of relationships (e.g. big—little; fat—lean; etc.).
   2. To learn to tell stories about pictures, events, etc.
   3. To learn to classify thoughts in an appropriate, orderly fashion.

E. Functional Reading
   1. To learn to read flash cards with functional words or simple sentences written on them.
   2. To learn to read a simple sentence from a chalkboard.

F. Writing
   1. To learn to copy words printed or written by the teacher on cards, posters, chalkboard, etc.
   2. To learn to write words independently.
   3. To learn to copy sentences printed or written by the teacher on cards, posters, chalkboard.
   4. To learn to print or write simple sentences independently.

IV. Mathematics Sequence

A. Discriminatory Concepts
   1. Quantity:
      a. few—many
      b. more—less
      c. lighter—heavier
   2. Position:
      a. tall—short
      b. front—behind
      c. on the side of
      d. on—off
      e. open—shut
   3. Measures:
      a. cupful
      b. pailfull, etc.
   4. Shapes:
      a. circle
      b. square
      c. triangle
      d. rectangle

B. Number Concepts

   1. To learn to recognize whole objects are the sum total of parts of objects.
   2. To learn the meaning of numbers (in relation to groups and objects).
   3. To learn to reproduce numbers on paper, cards, or chalkboards.

C. Arithmetic Sequences

   1. To learn to group objects in groups of twos, fives, tens, etc.
   2. To learn to do simple addition and subtraction.
   3. To learn to recognize fractions of the whole (e.g. halves or quarters of an object).
   4. To learn to use numbers to measure things (inch, foot, yard).

D. Time

   1. To learn why it is important to tell time.
   2. To learn to apply number concepts to the telling of time by the meaning of relative positions of the hands of a clock.
   3. To learn to tell time by the hours.
   4. To learn to tell time by the half hour.
   5. To learn to tell time by the quarter of an hour.
   6. To learn what a minute is.
   7. To learn to tell how many minutes before or after an hour it is.

E. Money

   Note: It is important that real money be used.

   1. To learn the value of different coins:
      a. penny to half-dollar.
      b. five pennies equal one nickel.
      c. five nickels equal one quarter.
      d. two quarters equal one half-a-dollar.
   2. To learn the value of different bills ($1-$100):
      a. five $1's = $5.
      b. two $5's = $10.
   3. To learn how to count coins.
   4. To learn how to make and give change.

V. Science

A. Origin of foods
   1. To learn that some foods come from trees, bushes, vines, etc.
   2. To learn that some foods come from underground.
   3. To learn that different parts of plants are edible.
   4. To learn the different seasonal foods.
   5. To learn the different kinds of meats.

B. Plant Life
   1. To learn that a plant reproduces and dies.
   2. To learn that plants give food, clothing, shelter, and decoration.
   3. To learn that some plants grow underground while others grow in the water.
   4. To learn the major parts of plants.
   5. To learn the functions of the major parts of plants.
   6. To learn that certain plants are harmful.
   7. To learn to discriminate between harmful and helpful plants.

C. Animal Life
   1. To learn to recognize familiar insects, birds, and animals.
   2. To learn that some animals are helpful.
   3. To learn that animals live on land, in trees, in caves, underground, and in water.
   4. To learn how animals travel (e.g. swim, crawl, fly, jump, etc.).

D. Signs of the Seasons of the Year
   (lightning, rainstorms, wind, snow, etc.)
   1. To learn to discriminate between the seasons:
      a. clothing worn
      b. activities of each
   2. To learn to associate the season with the appropriate months (i.e. when it starts, when it ends).

E. Weather
   1. To learn that there are different forms of weather.
   2. To learn how the different forms of weather are caused:
      a. wind
      b. temperature
      c. humidity, etc.
   3. To learn how we measure:
      a. temperature

  b. humidity

  c. wind, etc.

 4. To learn how rain, snow, sleet, and hail are formed.

F. Our Planet

 1. To learn that the earth is round.

 2. To learn the relationship between the earth, sun, moon, and stars.

 3. To become aware of certain geographical conditions such as mountains, forests, swamps, lakes, rivers, and oceans.

 4. To learn that there are certain resources that come from the earth such as oil, coal, iron, and diamonds.

 5. To learn how certain resources are used (e.g., coal, fuel, iron, steel, wood, lumber).

G. Sky Solar Bodies

 1. To learn the causes of daytime and nighttime (rotations of earth).

 2. To learn that the earth travels around the sun (revolutions of earth).

 3. To learn the different phases of the moon (full, 1st, 2nd, 3rd, quarter, etc.).

 4. To learn that a group of stars make a pattern and to know some familiar patterns (Little and Big Dipper, North Star, etc.).

VI. Sensory Concept Training

A. Visual

 1. To learn to identify different colors.

 2. To learn to discriminate between different colors.

 3. To learn to associate colors to objects.

 4. To learn to identify distances such as far—near, next to, etc.

 5. To learn to discriminate between distances such as far, near, next to, etc.

 6. To learn to associate distances.

 7. To learn to identify differences in objects such as big, biggest; small, smallest.

 8. To learn to discriminate between differences in objects such as big, biggest; small, smallest.

 9. To learn to associate differences in objects to sizes of objects.

B. Auditory
   1. To learn to identify various sounds which are pleasant and unpleasant.
   2. To learn to discriminate between sounds that are pleasant and unpleasant.
   3. To learn to associate pleasant and unpleasant sounds with objects.

C. Tactile
   1. To learn to identify specific textures of materials such as wool, silk, cotton, and flannel.
   2. To learn to discriminate between different specific textures of material.
   3. To learn to associate specific textures to different materials such as wool and sweater.
   4. To learn to identify objects with descriptive words such as sticky, rough, smooth, etc.
   5. To learn to discriminate objects with descriptive words such as sticky, rough, smooth, etc.
   6. To learn to associate objects with descriptive words such as sticky—candy; rough—sandpaper.

D. Gustatory
   1. To learn to identify similar taste of foods and liquids:
      a. warm—hot
      b. salty—saltier
      c. sweet—sweeter
      d. tart—sour
   2. To learn to discriminate between similar taste. (How are they different?)
   3. To learn to associate similar tastes to foods and liquids.

E. Olfactory
   1. To learn to identify odors which infer danger (gas, smoke).
   2. To learn to discriminate between odors which infer danger.
   3. To learn to associate odors which infer danger with objects or things they come from (e.g. gas—stove).

VII. Safety Habit Training

A. The Home
   1. To learn to use bannisters or guide rails while walking on stairs.

2. To learn how and when to use household tools or equipment:
   a. knives, forks, spoons
   b. stoves, sinks, refrigerators
   c. rakes, brooms, spades, hoes
3. To become aware of the dangers of hot objects:
   a. stoves
   b. water
   c. radiators
   d. cooking utensils, pots, pans, kettles, etc.
4. To become aware of the dangers of sharp instruments kept around the house and learn to avoid touching or raising them unless properly supervised:
   a. scissors
   b. razor blades
   c. lawn mowers
   d. rockers
   e. pitchforks or shovels
5. To learn to keep out of the household medicine cabinet and to know the dangers associated with it.
6. To learn not to touch or use cleaning substances or insecticides unless properly supervised.

B. The Community
   1. To learn the proper procedures when walking in the street:
      a. walk straight
      b. keep head up
      c. look where you are going (keep eyes open and off ground)
      d. keep away from cracks, holes, bumps, in the ground
      e. stay away from gutter
      f. step at corners
   2. To learn to recognize the safety signs and signals found in the community:
      a. stop sign
      b. traffic light
      c. railroad crossing
      d. sirens (fire, police, ambulance)
   3. To learn to avoid obvious dangers such as empty lots, holes in the ground, and uncovered manholes.
   4. To learn to stay away from lakes, swamps or ponds found in one's community.
      a. Watch where you are going.
      b. No wandering.
      c. Avoid touching objects.

C. The School
   1. To learn to avoid accidents in the classroom by:
      a. learning proper standing and sitting positions
      b. learning to place one's chairs under the desks or table when leaving desk or table
      c. learning to place chair on top of desks before going home
      d. establishing safe and orderly behavior patterns
   2. To learn to perform properly during fire and air raid drills.
   3. To learn to establish safe behavior patterns on the playground or gym.
   4. To become aware of the safety of others in:
      a. the hall
      b. classroom
      c. playground, etc.

D. The Bus
   1. To learn to get on and off bus safely.
   2. To learn to listen to directions given by teacher, adults, or bus driver.
   3. To learn not to eat on the bus.
   4. To learn not to throw objects on to the floor of the bus (gum, paper, pencils, etc.).
   5. To learn not to throw objects out of the windows of the bus (gum, paper, objects, etc.).
   6. To learn to speak softly while on the bus.

VIII. Arts and Crafts

A. Personal Development
   1. To develop and encourage growth and individuality through arts and crafts.
   2. To broaden one's leisure time by acquiring a hobby through arts and crafts.
   3. To develop a sense of accomplishment by the making of products through the use of arts and crafts.
   4. To encourage the use of materials in creative ways to express one's ideas and feelings.
   5. To gain satisfaction from handling and experimenting with materials.

B. Occupational Skills Development
   1. To gain satisfaction from seeing one's work progress, whether for decoration or useful purposes, for home or school.

2. To learn to complete a particular task or project.
3. To develop the ability to work in a cooperative manner in groups or as individuals.
4. To learn to be accurate in using media.
5. To learn to be accurate in the use of tools.
6. To learn to be neat and orderly when using tools and media.
7. To learn to follow a plan or procedure in its proper order.
8. To learn to make individual choices in choosing tools, materials, and projects.
9. To learn to develop taste and judgment by making choices in size, color, form, and textures.

C. Gross Motor Control

To develop muscular control of the gross muscles through the development of certain skills.

1. To learn to grasp large areas or objects.
2. To learn to release large areas or objects.
3. To learn to hold large areas or objects.
4. To learn to punch large areas or objects.
5. To learn to push large areas or objects.
6. To learn to pull large areas or objects.
7. To learn to press large areas or objects.
8. To learn to pound large areas or objects.
9. To learn to twist large areas or objects.

D. Fine Motor Control

To develop muscular control of the fine muscles through the development of certain skills:

1. To learn to grasp small areas or objects.
2. To learn to release small areas or objects.
3. To learn to develop thumb-index coordination.
4. To learn how to hold different object.
5. To learn how to pinch.
6. To learn how to push.
7. To learn how to pull.
8. To learn how to press.
9. To learn how to pound.
10. To learn how to twist.

IX. Physical Education

A. Competitive Games

1. To learn to cooperate with others.

2. To learn to develop endurance.
3. To learn to listen to and follow directions.
4. To learn leadership qualities.
5. To learn to work for a team or group.

B. Calisthenics
   1. To increase one's stamina and breath control.
   2. To learn to improve one's posture.
   3. To learn to bend, roll, skip, hop, march, run, etc.
   4. To learn to develop self-discipline.

C. Activities for Healthy Physical Development
   1. Mat activities
      a. To develop arm, neck, stomach muscles for good posture.
      b. To gain a better sense of timing.
      c. To overcome any awkward body movements.
   2. Rope Exercises
      a. To gain better gross and fine muscle coordination.
      b. To gain a better sense of timing.
      c. To increase one's coordination.

D. Gross Motor Skills
   1. To learn to develop better gross motor coordination through the use of competitive games by
      a. running
      b. throwing
      c. jumping
      d. kicking
      e. racing
      f. catching
      g. bouncing
      h. pulling
   2. To learn to develop gross motor skills through the use of calisthenics by
      a. walking
      b. marching
      c. running
      d. bending
      e. twisting
      f. jumping
      g. rolling
      h. sliding
      i. hopping

j. lifting
k. pulling

E. Fine Motor Skills
   1. To learn to develop fine motor coordination through the use of competitive games by
     a. grasping
     b. releasing
     c. holding
     d. catching
   2. To learn to develop fine motor coordination through the use of calisthenics by
     a. grasping
     b. releasing
     c. finger exercises
     d. hand exercises
     e. foot and leg exercises
   3. To develop coordination of bodily movements through rhythm and tempo:
     a. clapping
     b. stamping
     c. swaying
     d. walking
     e. dancing (square, ballroom)
     f. running (trot, gallop)
     g. marching

X. Cultural Appreciation

A. Music
   1. To learn to recognize the different types of musical instruments.
   2. To learn to play rhythm band instruments (drum, tom-tom, stick, jingle-bell, symbols, sandblocks, tambourine, triangle, and tone blocks).
   3. To learn that musical instruments can produce different sounds, rhythms, and tempos.
   4. To learn to reproduce different rhythms and tempos by using band instruments, dancing, marching, clapping, and singing.
   5. To encourage enjoyment and appreciation of music by
     a. singing
     b. dancing
     c. listening to phonograph and radio

d. participation in musical performances (plays, chorale, singing)

B. Art
1. To learn to control movements within a prescribed area to create better art forms.
2. To learn to recognize and to seek beauty through art.
3. To develop creativity and imagination through the various art forms.
4. To learn to appreciate famous paintings (Mona Lisa, Blue Boy, etc.).
5. To learn to appreciate other types of art (sculpture, photography, tapestry, metal crafts, etc.).

C. Dancing
1. To learn to discriminate between the different types of dances.
2. To learn to associate different types of dances with different types of music.
3. To learn to enjoy the beauty of dancing and dance steps.

D. Literature
1. To learn to listen to good literature.
2. To learn to dramatize a story.
3. To learn to become familiar with poetic forms.
4. To learn to recite poetry.
5. To learn to become familiar with stories and poems that are part of our American heritage.

PERCEPTUAL AND MOTOR SKILLS TRAINING

I. Perceptual Training

A number of perceptual areas are individually evaluated and interpolated into appropriate remedial programming. Ancillary services specialists meet with small groups of youngsters, and scheduled classroom demonstration lessons are offered by the program specialist. The perceptual areas include the following:

A. Visual
1. Visual Identification
2. Visual Discrimination
3. Visual Memory
4. Visual Association

    5. Visual Verbal Labelling
    6. Visual Verbal Description
    7. Visual Comprehension

B. Auditory
    1. Auditory Discrimination
    2. Auditory Memory
    3. Auditory Association
    4. Auditory Verbal Association
    5. Auditory Verbal Labelling
    6. Auditory Verbal Automatic Response
    7. Auditory Comprehension

C. Spatial Awareness

D. Spatial Memory

E. Self-Concept

F. Conversational Speech

II. Motor Skills Training

Our *motor skills* training program is also developmental in nature. Its sequence of learning skills is as follows:

A. Introductory Learning Skills
    1. Standing in the proper position for exercises:
      a. a straight line, one behind the other
      b. a circle, by holding hands
    2. Introduction to balancing bar
    3. Introduction to high bar
    4. Running by command
    5. The exercises:
      a. deep knee bends
      b. bending from the waist in different directions
      c. arm rotations
      d. introduction to parts of the body during exercises (head, knees, toes, etc.)
    6. Ball passing and simple catching
    7. Bicycle riding
    8. Hobbyhorse
    9. Use of ball during self-expression (recreation)

B. Elementary Learning Skills
    1. Exercises
        a. know parts of body by command (waist, legs, arms)
        b. running in place
    2. Line and circle games
        a. songs: "Farmer in the Dell" and many others
        b. ball passing and throwing with each other
        c. relays (with balls, pegs, and bars)
        d. use of leaders in multi-line games (using single lines)
    3. Tumbling and mat activities
        a. forward roll
        b. wrestling
    4. High bar
        a. self-chinning
        b. forward roll with help
        c. climbing and swinging from bar
    5. Running
        a. boys and girls in competitive running
        b. with and for objects
        c. replacing objects in proper positions
    6. Bicycle riding (around obstacles)
    7. Self-expression through
        a. use of balls
        b. bicycles
        c. high bar
        d. balancing bar
    8. Balance bar (walking by self)

C. Intermediate Learning Skills
    1. Exercises
        a. use of all parts of the body by number association and routines
        b. demonstrations by youngsters standing in front of a group and leading others.
        c. running together on command
    2. Balancing bars
        a. walking by self with proper footing
        b. introducing walking the bar backwards
    3. High bar
        a. chinning (self)
        b. forward rolls (self)
        c. legs hanging

4. Circle and line formation
New games: dodge ball, "catch me", kick ball by teams, Indian club relays, ball catching in competitions, relays

5. Basket shooting
   a. one hand push shot
   b. two hand set shot
   c. introduction in dribbling

D. Advanced Learning Skills
   1. Exercises (all parts of the body by command)
   2. Throwing balls for distance and accuracy (fire ball, hit the peg)
   3. Running to obtain speed and agility (potato races, base running, straight relays for competition)
   4. Catching (softballs, footballs, whiffel ball games, pass and receiving)
   5. High bar (self-chinning, rolls, leg hands)
   6. Balance bar (primarily for those who need the work, forward, backwards, pivoting on the bar and then walk back)
   7. Tumbling and mat activities (rolls, forward, backwards, simple head stand with help, wrestling for boys who are able)

Chapter 2

The Pre-primary and Primary Special Classes for the Educable Retardate

Evelyn Farrell

INTRODUCTION

The pre-primary and primary class is for children who are considered educable retardates (I.Q. 50-75). For some of them it is their first school experience. The class provides a structured environment in which they can form satisfactory peer relationships and achieve a degree of success in initial school experiences.

The goal of the class is to provide each child with the learning situations that will meet his individual needs. In order to accomplish this goal, most instruction is on an individual basis. Occasionally, it is possible to give instruciton to small groups of three or four. Group instruction is usually confined to the curriculum areas of science and social studies. Here, the teacher can provide experiences, both real and vicarious that will be meaningful to the group.

Many of these young children have perceptual, speech, and motor control problems. The children require specific help in overcoming their difficulties *before any of the usual curriculum areas can be explored.* Also, the children receive speech therapy for articulation problems and participate in the music and physical education programs.

The materials and activities suggested here are functional. Pragmatically, they have "worked." In many of the curriculum areas there is a wide range of material to be used, but it often must be altered and modified to meet the needs of these children. The teacher constantly seeks new methods and materials to augment those in use and explores them fully to benefit these children who cannot learn without special help.

The major objectives of the pre-primary class, therefore, are to provide an environment for each child that will foster a feeling of security and accomplishment and provide the opportunity for maturation through self-help.

SELF-HELP AND PERCEPTION

Primarily, these very young children come to school in a rather helpless state insofar as self-help is concerned. Usually they are accustomed to having their mothers do mostly everything for them; therefore, their ability to take care of themselves in a large social environment, such as a public school represents, is completely undeveloped. They need special help in learning to care for themselves so that one of the first things to be considered is teaching them to be able to help themselves. In other words, they come to school unable to unbutton or unzipper their clothing or take off their boots, so they must be taught to do these things.

A major phase of helping them to maintain themselves in school is to teach them to get along with other people. It is both an immediate goal and a long-range one. These children have to learn self-control and how to follow rules. They become a part of the peer group within the classroom and a part of the overall school. Such concepts as sharing and responsibility can be initiated from the first day. This training is probably the most important one that we undertake in teaching the child to take his place in society. We cannot confine ourselves solely to intellectual development, because the child has to function first as a person.

The following charts show the concrete steps necessary for introducing self-help and perception training. The units are listed first, followed by the activities which the teacher engages in, and finally a last column indicates the materials most helpful for teaching the unit. This particular breakdown is followed throughout this book.

TABLE 1

SELF-HELP AND PERCEPTION TRAINING

Units	Activities	Materials
I. Clothing		

A. Undressing
1. ability to unbutton or unzip outer garment
2. ability to take off coat or sweater (including over the head)
3. ability to remove boots and/or shoes (unless tied with double bow)
	A. The activities in this area are performed by the child as the occasion arises and mostly with his own clothes. Time is taken to help each child depending on his needs until he has achieved independence and can help himself and, on occasion, another less able than himself.	"All By Herself"
		"All By Himself"
		  Creative Playthings
		  Princeton, New Jersey
		
		"Five (5) Dressing Frames": Snapping
		  Zipper
		  Shoe Lacing
		  Large Button
		  Bow Tying

B. Dressing
1. putting on coat, smock, or sweater
2. fastening (buttons, zippers, snaps)
3. putting on boots, shoes, sneakers
4. tying laces and bows
	B. While there are devices that can be used for the various operations of fastening garments, experience has proven that the most profitable learning experience is for the child to learn on himself. Recommendation is made to the parents to provide clothing with large, simple fasteners or buttons.	Creative Playthings
		Princeton, New Jersey
		
		"Lacing Boot"
		  Creative Playthings
		  Princeton, New Jersey
		
		special frames with zippers, buttons, snaps, etc.

C. Use of handkerchief 1. awareness of need 2. proper use		

TABLE 1 (*Continued*)
SELF-HELP AND PERCEPTION TRAINING

Units	Activities	Materials
II. Responsibility		
A. For self and others	A. Hooks are provided for children unable to use hangers then children are taught how to use hangers.	Pegboard with hooks
1. hanging clothing		
2. keeping desks in order	Watching and recognition of his name and eventually recognizing other children's names.	Space is set aside for labelling own name; children have name tages taped on desks and also one that is free to match against taped ones.
3. respect for others' belongings		
4. putting class things away in proper place	No new activity is begun until all material from previous activity is put away in proper place.	
	Teacher helps with all activities until child is capable of performing task alone.	
B. Sharing and taking turns	B. Sharing and taking turns is stressed by the teacher and imposed as rule until it becomes part of pattern.	
1. with equipment		
2. with teacher's attention		
3. in group games		
C. Independence	C. When a child reaches this stage he is encouraged to try new and more difficult tasks: hanging up clothes, taking out pencils and crayons, getting paper from shelf, going to office, etc.	Using a check-off list as child succeeds in mastering each activity (e.g. after an errand or using bathroom facilities).
1. to do routine task		
2. go on simple errands		
3. use of bathroom	Since school lavatory facilities are often different from home, actual instruction in proper use is necessary.	

TABLE 1 (*Continued*)

SELF-HELP AND PERCEPTION TRAINING

Units	Activities	Materials
III. Good Manners		
A. To peer group and adults	A. Good manners are stressed in every activity whether verbal or action. Use of correct names, speaking quietly, consideration of others, and good manners when eating are a part of everyday routine.	
1. "magic words"—please and thank-you		
2. respect		
	1. Set up a daily exercise when children *can* say good morning to each other.	
	2. Using toy table, the children can set up utensils and enjoy "meals" together.	
B. On telephone	B. Activities on the telephone During free playtime or in structured role play activities, have the children call someone on the phone and talk.	toy telephone or "tele-trainer" from telephone company most useful when available
1. speak clearly		
2. for short time—don't "hog" the telephone		
IV. *Perception Training**		
A. Development of self-image	A. Have child learn rhymes and songs about self (e.g. "I Have Two Eyes to See With"); use mirror and make faces showing happiness, sadness, anger, etc.	*Rhymes for Fingers and Flannelboards* Louise Binder Scott and J. J. Thompson Webster Publishing Co., 1960.
1. body image		
2. emotional reactions		
3. sensory perception (how things feel, taste, smell, etc.)	Finger-plays for parts of body; make pie-plate face with cut out parts.	

* Perception training is also given in language preparation later on.

TABLE 1 *(Continued)*
SELF-HELP AND PERCEPTION TRAINING

Units	Activities	Materials
B. Directionality (including laterality)	B. Have child connect dots on blackboard from left to right. Use a cardboard with a cutout section. Mount a small object (toy animal, car, plane) and have child pull object from left to right by a small attached string.	
C. Form and space	C. Have child duplicate teacher-made pattern with blocks, pegs, and beads. Have children make own block buildings.	
D. Motor coordination 1. gross motor control 2. fine motor control, including eye-hand coordination	D. Walk on line Skip, hop, jump Bounce and catch ball Throw and catch ball Build with blocks, string beads Puzzles, prepunched sewing cards Pegs in pegboard, tracing, coloring, cutting	

ARITHMETIC

Some of the children who come in have been exposed to some kindergarten so that they have had an exposure to number work in the kindergarten area. Others come directly from home. In some of the homes there is an attempt made at some number work, but for the most part the children come in without any basic knowledge or concept of numbers as such. Even the rote counting is very poor. They will count 1, 2, 4—having heard older brothers or sisters say numbers, but they have no concept of the sequence of numbers. Therefore, we start with rote counting so that they know the sequence of the numbers. We also do this with rhymes, little jingles, and with the Mother Goose type thing that has been in use for years.

The children need a very concrete type of work in the development of the number concepts and we start this by counting in a one-to-one relationship all the things that are familiar to them: families, the people in the room, the objects that we touch and come in contact with, etc. We then go into the perception of and development of number concepts. Actually, we are focusing on understanding what a group is and what it means.

After the concept has been developed, we work on the recognition of symbols that represent quantities. We practice writing and recognizing the number symbols. The ability of the children to recognize (the extent to which they are able to recognize) symbols depends on how far they are able to go in their development of the numbers.

When we start getting into other areas such as a concept of time, it is done very generally. We talk about night and day, about a time to eat, a time to sleep, and a time to get up and come to school. Usually the best we can do is to tell time to the nearest hour on the clock, but for the most part it is a very general concept of time.

Quantitative concepts are developed at a later period after the concept of numbers. We do talk about things that are "more and less." We talk about large groups of things always using concrete materials. We can do some work with fractions, e.g. what is a half? But for the most part, it is a general type of concept development.

Qualitative concepts can be developed a little bit further than that. With concrete materials we can actually develop the concepts of such things as size and shape, place concepts such as over, under, and in, and the usual type of vocabulary that accompanies such concepts. We can do it in a very concrete way for the children to understand. For example we can talk about money because they all have experience with it. They bring money to school for milk. They are aware that their mother pays the ice-cream man money. (They are not quite so aware of the amount of money spent in the supermarket.) But we teach them to recognize coins like a penny, a nickel, and a dime. We count out pennies and we play store with the idea of exchanging money for material.

When we have had the children for a longer time, we can sometimes get to subtraction as such. Of course, in developing a concept of numbers you are in a sense teaching subtraction at a concrete level. However, the actual process of subtraction is a difficult one for the children to understand so only the more children and those whom we have had for a longer period of time are able to do this.

Arithmetic concepts are developed slowly and are continuously reinforced through practice and drill until they are fully understood. We try to show the child just how arithmetic in all of its various phases is so much a part of his everyday life and how much he will need it in the future if he is to be a contributing member in our society.

TABLE 2
NUMBERS

Units	Activities	Materials
I. Rote Counting (learning to count in order)	I. Games, rhymes, jingles Finger-plays	
II. Counting in a One-to-one Relationship	II. Counting boys and girls; desks and chairs; paper; crayons; milk; straws; or candles on cake for each year	"5" stack counting frame pegs and pegboard "Beaded Pressure Sensitive Numbers" Webster Paper & Supply Co. Albany, New York
III. Preliminary Development of Number Concepts (pre-primary to primary)	III. Groupings of children Flannelboard activities Concrete objects of various items (boys, girls, trains, fruits) Finding pictures of a given number of objects Counting to 10—forwards and backwards Rote counting from 1 to 100 by 1's, 5's and 10's Which number precedes 25? Which follows 25? or any number. Simple addition and subtraction: $3+1=4$, $9-5=4$, etc. Simple problems given orally by teacher	bead rods arithmetic kits (teacher-made) colored cubes felt cutouts die-cut rubber sets giant dominoes perception cards "Kinesthetic Numbers in a Box" and "Kinesthetic Numbers on a Board" Creative Playthings, Inc. Princeton, New Jersey "Numberite" The Judy Company Minneapolis, Minnesota "Number-Jumble" The Judy Company Minneapolis, Minnesota

TABLE 2 (*Continued*)
NUMBERS

Units	Activities	Materials
IV. Recognition and Writing of Number Symbols	IV. Observe symbols in familiar places (classroom door, house, clock, supermarket) Matching symbols Tracing symbols	die-cut rubber numbers felt cut-outs "Pattern Board" Creative Playthings, Inc. Princeton, New Jersey
V. Concept of Time (i.e. time to eat, sleep, go home, get up, etc.) *Goal:* possibly to tell time to nearest hour.	V. Call attention to clock as various activities occur Discuss routine of day in school and at home Telling time to the hour; the half hour Children make own clocks from paper plates	*Good Morning-Good Night* Frank Luther (Wonder Books) Grosset "Timmy Time Clock Puzzle" Ben-G Products East Williston, New York
VI. Quantitative Concepts	VI. Develop vocabulary (one half, more, less, few, many, bigger, smaller, etc.) Demonstrate with concrete materials	Instructor Kindergarten-Primary numerical relations

TABLE 2 *(Continued)*
NUMBERS

Units	Activities	Materials
VII. Qualitative Concepts (ex. size, shape, place—over, under) *Goal:* to gear your demands realistically to their level.	VII. Matching objects by size and/or shape Finding familiar objects with same shape as one shown Guessing games of where something is placed in relation to another Introducing geometric forms such as circle, square, etc.	*Ups and Downs* and *The Size of It* Ethel S. Berkley E. M. Hale & Co., Wisconsin *Shapes* Miriam Schlein William Scott, Inc., New York, 1952
VIII. Money	VIII. Recognition of penny, nickel, dime, quarter Counting out pennies for milk Playing store Making change Count a handful of pennies, nickels, dimes	actual money resource material Teacher's Guide "Math Workshop for Children" Robert Wirtz and Morton Botel *Rhymes for Fingers and Flannelboards* Louise Binder Scott and J. J. Thompson Webster Publishing Co., 1960

SCIENCE

The development of science with these children is done, of course, at a very elementary level and at all times the experience of the children is taken into account. If they come to school without many experiences we try to provide real experiences for them. When this is impossible, we use audio-visual aids such as movies, filmstrips, records, and pictures from magazines. We thus try to provide vicarious experiences to augment the real experience, if possible.

Some of the first steps involve recognition of animals. The first ones they are familiar with, of course, are their own pets. When possible we visit a local farm to see farm animals. We have never taken them to the circus although they have been to the zoo. They are aware of some of the woodland creatures that they see about: the squirrels, chipmunks, birds, etc. We try to teach safety with the animals as well as recognition. We develop the theme that animals are different. (Some have four legs and run; birds fly; and fish live under the water. There are other kinds of animals too that resemble snakes and these have no legs at all.) The next area that comes within their experience is the weather which is a continuing unit. As each season arrives we talk about it. This is not developed as one unit but rather as a continuing unit that can stop for a time and then be picked up again as the seasons change.

Many plants can be kept in the room and we can plant seeds and grow flowers with the children so that we talk about plants and how we take care of them. They are very interested in how they grow, so we can take one of the plants apart and show them that it is made up of parts. We plant seeds and then see how they grow to look like the plant that we had to start with. It gives them an idea of growing things, and they enjoy the esthetic quality of the plants as well.

TABLE 3
SCIENCE

Units	Activities	Materials

I. Recognition of Animals
A. Kinds
  1. pets
  2. farm animals
  3. wild animals
    a. circus
    b. zoo
    c. woodland creatures
B. Classes
  1. four-legged
  2. birds
  3. fish
  4. others (frogs, snakes, etc.)
	I. Discuss pets children have
	Utilize children's experiences on trips to farm, zoo, circus
	Take class trip to local zoo, farm, nature walk
	Classification (e.g. dogs, big-little; long-haired, spotted, different colors)
	Make scrapbook
	Color ditto sheets
	Filmstrips
	Read animal stories
	Keep fish tank (live animals and birds present too great problem of classroom management with these young children e.g. raising guppies)
	Make bird-feeding station
		magazine pictures for bulletin board
		I Like Animals
		Dahlov Ipcar
		Alfred A. Knopf, Inc.
		New York, 1960
		The Second-Story Giraffe
		Jane Thayer
		William Morrow and Co.
		New York, 1959
		
		Dr. Frances R. Horwich and Reinald Werrenrath, Jr.
		Rand McNally and Co.
		Chicago, 1954
		Records: "Little White Duck," "Trip to the Farm," "Katie the Kangaroo," "Jimmy the Jolly Giraffe"

II. Weather
A. Seasons
  1. fall
  2. winter
  3. spring
  4. summer
	II. Discuss kinds of weather, how we dress, activities suitable to various weather situations
	Have calendar bulletin board on which kind of weather can be noted
	Make scrapbooks of family or children's activities for various times of year
		paper dolls of all family members with clothes for various weather
		weather chart
		Some Day
		Grace Paull
		Abelard-Schuman
		New York, 1957

TABLE 3 (*Continued*)
SCIENCE

Units	Activities	Materials
	Take walks to note what happens in seasons to animals, plants, neighbor's homes	*Winter Is Here*
		Spring Is Here
		Summer Is Here
	Read seasonal stories	*Autumn Is Here*
	Keep weather calendar	all published by Row Peterson
	Observe changes in temperature, loss of leaves from trees, etc.	Company
		"What Makes It Rain"—Decca Records
III. Plants and Flowers	III. Have children bring in real flowers	plants in classroom
A. Kinds	Have plants in room to show effects of watering, sun, etc.	pictures of flowers, trees, etc.
1. house plants	Plant flower, grass seed and bulbs.	
2. flowers	Root plant in water to show parts then plant	
3. shrubs and trees	Take walks at various times of year to see weather effects on plants	
B. How they grow		
1. parts		
2. needs		

HEALTH

The next big area, and this too is a continuing activity, is health. While we work in it as a unit, we also work on it day by day. We talk about nutrition, the various kinds of food, and our need for good food. In talking about the things that we need to stay healthy we also get involved with the proper way of eating things. We stress cleanliness of ourselves, our teeth, and our clothing. We talk about proper rest, and we have rest time each day to refresh ourselves. In fact, we have a quiet time after any great physical activity.

When we discuss taking care of ourselves and keeping ourselves healthy this is done on a very elementary level. For example, we stress daily the importance of not putting things into our mouths, of not touching our eyes, or putting objects near our eyes or ears. We always stress the need for them to listen to what their mother says about walking in the water and doing what the doctor tells them when they are ill.

SAFETY

Here, again, we have a continuing unit that starts in September and goes right through to June. It too is stressed day by day. Safety in school is discussed, emphasizing how we behave, how we follow rules, how we use equipment on the playground, and how we behave in the classroom. We stress the need for them to be very careful on their way to school; how to avoid going out into the road where there are automobiles, and how to behave on the bus. To develop a respect for a policeman and for a safety patrol is also discussed.

We review safety at home as well and we try to do this by noting which things are safe to handle. Thus we try to stress the positive and the preventative rather than the overwhelming dangers that would frighten them, while at the same time still teaching them respect for things that could hurt them.

TABLE 4
HEALTH AND SAFETY

Units	Activities	Materials

I. Health
A. Nutrition
  1. kinds of foods
  2. need for good foods
    a. for growth
    b. for good health
  3. proper way to eat
	I. Bulletin board of basic foods
	Grouping foods
	Growth charts
	Records of new teeth
	Visit to nurse and dental hygienist
	Morning inspection
	Use playhouse to set good meal at table with toy foods; stress good table manners.
		health posters and pictures (not too complex)
		materials provided by nurse and dental hygienist
		soap
		mirror
		tissues
		hangers and hooks for clothing
		smocks to cover clothes for messy activities
		charts (put real toothbrush, tooth-paste, bar of soap, etc. on chart)
		Kellogg Breakfast Unit, Battle Creek, Michigan

B. Cleanliness
  1. self
    a. washing before eating
    b. after toilet
  2. teeth
  3. clothing
	Supervise hand washing
	Provide snack and rest time
	
	A daily health check to supplement this:	

C. Rest
  1. bedtime
  2. quiet time after physical activity
	1. play quiet music
	2. read stories
		Record: "Health Can Be Fun"
		Frank Luther
		charts, appropriate pictures

D. Care of body
(very elementary)
  1. not putting things in mouth
  2. not walking in puddles
  3. obeying doctor when ill
  4. keeping objects away from eyes and ears
	Children will need reminders in context as situations arise, e.g., rainy days discuss puddles.	

TABLE 4 (*Continued*)
HEALTH AND SAFETY

Units	Activities	Materials
I. Safety		
A. In school	Establish rules	Record: "Song of Safety"
1. walking	Constant practice	Frank Luther
2. following directions	Demonstration of use of equipment	
3. safe use of equipment	(pencils, scissors, etc.)	
a. on playground		
b. in classroom (with pencils and scissors)		
B. On way to school	Use play equipment to set up safe	safety posters
1. respect for police and safety patrol	situations of traffic control	
2. dangers of autos	Meet safety patrol and school crossing guards	
3. conduct on bus	Meet bus driver	
a. quiet so driver can hear		
b. sit in seat to avoid falling		
c. keep school bags on floor		
d. arms and heads inside window		
C. At home	Discussion on a very elementary level.	*Do You Know*
1. avoid hot things (water, pots, stove)	Some pictures may be possible to use but care must be taken. Use a hot plate.	Kay Ware and Gertrude B. Hoffsten, The Steck Co., 1962.
2. avoid sharp things (knives, forks, scissors)	Make popcorn, cocoa, etc. that they do not become too frightened. Cooperation	"First Steps to Health and Safety" Gale Smith
3. holding stair rail	with home a must to provide vicarious	Benton Review Publishing Co.
4. keeping paths and stairs clear	experiences.	

TABLE 4 (*Continued*)
HEALTH AND SAFETY

Units	Activities	Materials
5. stay away from open windows	Try to stress the positive and the preventative.	"Living Today"
6. do not wander away from home		Cole, Cole & Appleyard
7. avoid strangers	Make each child a large cardboard telephone with his phone number. Match their number from other cards.	McCormick-Mathers Publishing Co.
8. learn name, address, and telephone number		Instructor—Primary
		Science Concept Charts
9. avoid fires (matches, candles)	Use real phones (Kit from Phone Co.) which they can dial and which ring.	F. A. Owen Publishing Company
		Teleprompter Kit from phone co.

LANGUAGE ARTS

The language arts program is perhaps the most important of all the curriculum activities; it may be called the oral communication areas. These children need to develop the ability to speak and listen. Many of them come in speaking incoherently; they use baby talk and their speech is completely unclear. These children need to learn the words that identify what they do and the names of objects; in other words they need the ability to be able to communicate their needs in ways other than pantomine. Simply they need to learn how to use words. They have daily help to develop correct usage of words, and they learn how to say "I" instead of "me." They learn how to say the word "yes" instead of nodding their heads up and down, and they learn how to listen and follow very simple directions of perhaps two or three words.

This program starts out with just a one-to-one relationship with the teacher. Later they can listen when they are in a small group, and eventually they are able to listen when they are in a large group situation, e.g. in a fire drill, when a direction is given they can follow it as well as any of the other children in the building.

Where the existence of a major speech problem requires speech therapy, this is provided by the speech department. Through individual speech therapy they can eliminate many articulation problems or at least correct them to the very maximum that is possible. In order to do this of course we work on the development of skills. The first skill area that is developed is the auditory. They start out by learning to recognize familiar sounds and familiar voices. They learn the quality of sounds and how to listen to nursery rhymes and jingles. They listen to stories until they are able to repeat the main idea. After a while they get to be able to tell you something about the character in the story and they can recall some of the detail. We play little games where they develop *the ability to recognize the beginning sounds,* all on an auditory level. This precedes any reading skills that we may hope to develop at a later date. The children start telling stories from pictures, and they talk about events that happen one after the other.

After auditory skills are developed, the children develop *the ability to recognize objects by size, color, and shape.* They match like objects. They go from very simple things that are the same to more complex items. They develop the ability to discern differences in objects such as size, color, shape, orientation, and internal differences. Ultimately, they will learn the recognition of symbols; the first one, of course, which they come to is their own name. Later they will recognize any pertinent signs that they would meet such as stop signs, danger signs, and so on.

Eventually we get through the alphabet and, where possible, develop a sight vocabulary preliminary to starting an actual developmental reading program. We continually work on the emphasis of left to right, because all reading and writing that we do is done in a left to right orientation. They learn organization skills such as classification. They learn to find something that is missing. We work on sequence development. We continually review sensory perception in visual areas, auditory areas, tactile, and kinesthetic areas. When possible, we try to develop interpretative skills with them such as determining an emotional reaction and predicting outcomes and forming judgments. We work on motor skills, particularly to help them with their tracing, coloring, copying, and writing.

TABLE 5
LANGUAGE ARTS

Units	Activities	Materials
I. Oral Communication		
A. Speaking	A. Child encouraged to use words instead of gestures	children's own experiences
1. ability to communicate needs	Correct names for objects used	Show and Tell
2. ability to speak understandably	Vocabulary extended through pictures and actual objects or experiences	Ideal Action Pictures
3. increase vocabulary		Ideal Name Pictures
4. develop correct usage		"Instructo"—illustrated verbs and illustrated prepositions
5. ability to share ideas, fears, pleasures	Child encouraged to use sentences	
6. practice in good manners, (thank you, please, etc.)	Correct pronouns emphasized in all language activities	
B. Listening	Correct verb forms encouraged	Stories, poems, records used for listening activities. (If not available teacher can make her own tapes on tape recorder, using tapes of actual sounds reproduced on tape recorder.)
1. ability to understand and follow directions	Descriptive vocabulary encouraged (ex. adjectives, adverbs)	
2. ability to listen	Riddles and rhymes	
a. in one-to-one relationship	Choral speaking	
b. in small group situation		
c. in large group situation		
II. Development of Skills		
A. Auditory	A. Note familiar sounds:	rhythm band instruments
1. recognizing familiar sounds	1. at home	Peabody Language Development Kit
2. recognizing familiar voices	2. in school	American Guidance Service
3. identifying quality of sounds (high-low, loud-soft)	3. outdoors (e.g., car, plane)	Minneapolis, Minnesota
4. listening to nursery rhymes and repetitive jingles	4. animal sounds	Mother Goose stories, songs, records
	5. musical instruments	children's books either brought from home or obtained from library
	Games with children hiding eyes and listening to sound or voice	

TABLE 5 (*Continued*)
LANGUAGE ARTS

Units	Activities	Materials

5. listening to stories
  a. able to repeat main idea
  b. able to tell something of characters
  c. ability to recall some detail
	Games using pitch or loudness—instruments or clapping
	Have children learn nursery rhymes to repeat or sing in unison
	Listening to stories
	  1. stories read by teacher
	  2. experiences of other children
	  3. stories on records
	Have children act out story
	Children retell story in own words
	Draw pictures of stories
		flannelboard characters
		puppets of familiar characters

6. recognizing rhyming pairs
7. recognition of some beginning sounds
8. ability to tell stories from pictures
9. ability to relate events in sequence
	Children fill in word in rhyme:
	  1. known rhyme
	  2. teacher-made rhyme
	    (ex. birds fly high, in the ——)
	Children note other children's names that start the same
	Children tell story from a single picture; from a group of pictures
		pictures from magazines, coloring books, sample readiness books
		"Quees"
		  The Judy Company
		  Minneapolis, Minnesota

B. Visual 1. ability to recognize objects by color, size, and shape	Use concrete dimension objects to show likenesses and differences Use flat two dimensional representations of likenesses and differences Use pictures Use outline of geometric shapes (from simple to more complicated)	teacher-made devices flannelboard ideal picture charts name charts size charts alike and different "what's missing"

TABLE 5 (Continued)
LANGUAGE ARTS

Units	Activities	Materials
2. ability to match like objects from simple to more complex	Play matching games	"Kiddie Kards"
3. ability to discern differences from gross, differences to finer, and differences in:	1. at flannelboard	Antioch Bookplate Company Yellow Springs, Ohio
	2. dominoes	Reading Fun Puzzle # 2
	3. lotto	"Ben-G-Educator"
a. color		"Matchettes"
b. size		The Judy Company
c. shape		Minneapolis, Minnesota
d. internal differences		picture dominoes
e. orientation		lotto games
		Montessori form-board
		inset puzzles
4. ability to recognize symbols:	Label all children's belongings	"Kiddie Kards"
a. own name	Label areas of room and bulletin boards	Antioch Bookplate Company Yellow Springs, Ohio
b. pertinent signs (ex. STOP, danger, lavatories)	Make replicas of pertinent signs	large fibre-board signs (usual traffic symbols)
c. other's names	Display alphabet	large alphabet flash cards
d. alphabet	Take note of all signs as encountered	felt letters
e. initial sight vocabulary (a few of the older children may reach this phase of development)		kinesthetic letters

TABLE 5 (*Continued*)
LANGUAGE ARTS

Units	Activities	Materials
C. Left-to-Right	Demonstrate starting point in writing and reading	Reading Fun Puzzle # 3 "Ben-G-Educator"
1. emphasize starting all reading and writing activities on left	Note hand in "Pledge of Allegiance"	lotto
2. recognize left from right	Play hand games and learn rhymes for left and right	"Quees" The Judy Company Minneapolis, Minnesota picture cards
D. Organizational skills		
1. classification	Use playhouse to classify foods and/or objects	
a. broad class (e.g., things to eat)	Make bulletin board house, furnish rooms with appropriate pictures of furniture and objects used	
b. finer division (e.g., fruit)		
c. what's missing	Show outline pictures of familiar objects with something missing	
2. Sequence development	Use calendar for clothing and activities of various seasons and kinds of weather	
a. in story telling		
b. in picture arrangement		
3. Developing sensory perception		
a. visual		
b. auditory		
c. tactile		
d. kinesthetic		

TABLE 5 (*Continued*)
LANGUAGE ARTS

Units	Activities	Materials
E. Interpretive skills	Display pictures of faces showing various emotions	
1. determining emotional reactions	Use mirror to have children see own faces with various emotions	
2. reasoning prior happenings	Guide reactions by relating story happenings to children's own experiences	
3. predicting outcomes	Have children recall own reactions	
4. forming judgments	Have each child answer "What would happen" question	
F. Motor skills	Have children trace simple outlines or patterns	parquetry blocks
1. tracing	Stress coloring within lines	felt and kip letters
2. coloring	Use kinesthetic material for child to feel form	teacher-made dittoes
3. copying		
4. writing		

WRITING

These young children have eye-head coordination problems which make writing difficult. However, they are anxious to write as it is a symbol of being grown-up and they seem to associate writing with accomplishment. To give them a feeling of success they are taught to write their own names (or sometimes just the first initial) before they are taught the alphabet.

At first, no great stress is placed on form or relative size, as long as the symbols are recognizable. Writing is kept large until sufficient coordination is developed to be able to control the quality of the writing.

Initial experiences in copying writing are made simple by having the material to be copied on the same sheet. Copying from the chalkboard is the last experience because of the difficulty of transferring what is seen in one place to the paper which is in another place and the difficulty of changing the focus of the eyes so constantly from board to paper.

After the children have developed a mental age of at least six and a half years, we consider them ready for the next level, the primary level. Here basic tool subjects are enlarged upon with entension of readiness work leading to further expansion of reading, language arts, arithmetic, social studies, etc.

Psychological testing, concomitant with teacher observations are important to help make the determination of adequate mental age before progressing to the next level. It is important at the next level, as at all further expansions of the program, to continue to find time to develop good social, vocational, and personal adjustment skills.

TABLE 6
WRITING

Units	Activities	Materials
I. Writing names	I. Trace name at chalkboard with colored chalk Trace over chalk name with large brush dipped in water Trace over pencil name on large easel paper with thinned tempera paint Trace over name teacher has written on paper: 1. in solid line 2. see written model and then copy Copy name from model 1. feel felt letters and then write 2. see writen model and then copy	large easel brush and water die-cut felt letters (commercial) die-cut cardboard letters (commercial) plastic letters (commercial) teacher-made letters of velour paper on kip light colors of tempera paint letters made of plasticene (teacher-made) letters cut into tablets of hardening clay (teacher-made) papier-mache letters (teacher-made) sandpaper letters both teacher-made and commercial
II. Developing the alphabet A. Straight line letters B. Slant line letters C. Circle letters D. Arc letters E. Combination letters	II. Use kinesthetic materials for child to feel configuration of letters Have child trace solid line letters Have child trace broken line letters Have child copy letters from paper teacher has done	kinesthetic materials listed above alphabet cards—individual letters and sequence cards large line (one inch) paper large primary pencils To accentuate lines on paper, teacher can use Magic Markers in various colors e.g. top line can be green to start, bottom line red to stop).

TABLE 6 (Continued)
WRITING

Units	Activities	Materials
III. Writing Letters in Sequence A. Two letters same size B. Two letters different size C. Three letters	III. Teacher writes letters on prelined paper for child to copy. Teacher displays completed paper for child to use as model. Initially teacher may use some marking on paper to show child where to begin.	teacher-prepared paper of several lines including solid and dotted lines so child may note proper relative placement of letters in sequence large lined chart paper for child to see as model
IV. Copying Words A. Written on same paper by teacher B. From chalkboard or chart	IV. Once child has mastered copying three letters, it follows that these can have meaning by introducing number and color words. Teacher may write words on chart paper or chalkboard for child to copy.	room decorations of signs, number and color cards written in same type letters child is being taught liner for chalkboard colored chalk (yellow and white sufficient) to provide contrast between guidelines and letters
V. Copying Sentences*	V. Sentences can be about weather, an item of interest or a special event	

* This is a culminating activity that is not always possible for pre-primary children

READING

As always our goal is to place the child on a level commensurate with his functioning ability. Reading can stimulate the child in his efforts for reward and praise as much as and probably even more than other tool subjects. The child *must* be allowed to progress at his own pace.

In the reading readiness program he is introduced to colors, similarities, differences, laterality, directionality, visual and auditory discrimination, small and large muscle and motor involvement, etc. Essentially, our aim is to carry him from basic geometric forms and letters to words and ultimate developmental reading. When his sight vocabulary has been sufficiently increased, he will move on to the pre-primer and primer levels. Phonics are an ongoing part of the reading program and are broadened and expanded upon as the child masters the reading process.

TABLE 7
READING

Units	Activities	Materials
I. Readiness Level		
A. Developing oral ability	A. Give simple directions orally for children to follow	Readiness Series (with workbooks) Scott, Foresman and Co.
	Children give oral interpretation of stories taken from records, simple pictures, filmstrips, etc.	Readiness Series Houghton-Mifflin
	Children play games: guessing riddles, choral speaking, "guess who," "which part is missing"	"Kindergraph" Follett Co. Chicago, Illinois
B. Developing listening ability	B. Familiarize children with rhymes, different beginning sounds, sounds in the environment, etc.	Dolch Games
	Children play games such as: let's match the shapes, the letters, the pictures; name the color; make up story from picture; memory object game;	*Shapes* M. Schlein W. R. Scott Inc., 1952
	telephone game; whose voice is that?; is the piano note high or low; do my words rhyme?	*Book of Riddles* ("Animal Riddles") and *More Riddles* Bennett Cerf Random House
C. Developing visual ability	C. Children learn to recognize: colors, familiar objects, own names, labels, signs, directional words, shapes, etc.	*Everything Has a Shape, Everything Has a Size* B. Kohn Prentice-Hall

TABLE 7 (*Continued*)
READING

Units	Activities	
II. Pre-Primer Level		
A. Developing oral and listening ability	A. Increase rhyming ability	*The Cat In The Hat; The Cat In The Hat Comes Back;*
	Follow the leader (Can you repeat what I say?)	*One Fish, Two Fish, Red Fish, Blue Fish* Dr. Seuss Random House
	Increase classifying ability	
	Increase recognition of initial consonant sounds	*Go Dog Go!* Philip D. Eastman Random House
	Increase ability to answer questions about material read	
	Show and tell	*The City-Country ABC* Walters (Doubleday)
	Reading emotions (Does he look happy?, sad?, etc.)	
B. Developing visual ability	B. Increase ability to classify words, classify pictures, illustrate action pictures, recognize sight words, recognize word families	The Early I Can Read Books-Harper Bros.
	Play games such as: word bingo, word lotto, dominoes, checkers, etc.	phonic wheel (teacher-made)
		Glenn Learns To Read C. and M. Appell Duell, Sloane and Pierce, Co.

TABLE 7 *(Continued)*
READING

Units	*Activities*	*Materials*
III. Primer Level (adding additional skills)	III. Maintain and extend previous skills	*The True Book of Sounds We Hear* Podendorf Childrens Press
	Increase reading speed and comprehension	
	Understand more complex series of directions	
	Substitute initial consonants (box to fox)	Animal ABC Piatti Atheneum
	Recognizing opposites	*ABC Book* C. B. Falls Doubleday
	Adding endings (s, es, ed, er, etc.)	
	Recognizing simple compound words (into, upon, etc.)	
	Recognizing simple punctuation marks (period, comma, question mark, exclamation point)	Science Research Associates: Lab 1A—Listening Skills Builders and Power Builder Program
	Play games such as memory span, sound lotto, word bingo, scrambled sentences, retelling	Reading Lab IV/1 Reading Lab 1—
	a mixed up story in proper sequence	Word Games (Phonics)

SOCIAL STUDIES

The area of social studies draws primarily upon children's experiences. In the beginning of the year we start out with a unit which can be called "Orientation to School." School is a very large environment quite different from the home. We spend much time in developing an orientation to the physical surroundings and adjustment to the peer group as well as meeting the staff of the school where they are in contact with many adults as opposed to one or two in a family. We learn to conform to the rules and follow the social procedure that is expected of a person in a public environment. We establish the routine of the day which is different from the complete freedom of home. We have a definite time for all of our activities, and we have demands made upon us because we are sharing our time and our place with others. Thus we learn to work when it is work time, play when it is playtime and to put things away and take care of things that do not belong to us.

The next area that we involve ourselves in is developing a unit on the family. This is the area in which the children have now had all their experiences; they are aware of the people in their own family. They need to be helped a little bit on relationships with someone other than their mother and father. They learn about the fact that mother does work in the home by taking care of children. They all know that their fathers go out to work and we talk about some of the various kinds of things that fathers do when they are working. We talk about how fathers also work at home to help the family. We involve ourselves in ways that the children can help as well. Here it very often is helpful to have conferences with the family to give them suggestions on how they can let the children help to become more self-sufficient and feel they are more a part of the family unit.

We discuss our homes and the kind of a house we live in and what the rooms of the house are. We talk of neighbors who help us and neighbors in school who help us and whom we try to help. We talk about the other people in the community that help, namely the community helpers such as the policeman, the fireman, the mailman, and the merchants, whom they would meet when they go to the store with their mothers, and the doctor, who cares for them when they are ill.

During the course of the year we also mention the various holidays that come along. Some have historical significance and we try to go into a little background material in a very elementary level, so that the children can appreciate some of the things that are going on. Finally, there are the days that are just fun like Halloween, Christmas, and St. Valentine's Day; the children appreciate these too.

TABLE 8
SOCIAL STUDIES

Units	Activities	Materials
I. Orientation to School		
A. To physical surroundings	A. Show areas in classroom and explain uses Explore school building	
B. To peer group	B. Arrange small groups for shared activities Play "how do you do" games	
C. To staff of school	C. Visit various personnel; principal, secretaries, nurse, dental hygienist, custodians, cafeteria ladies Read stories of how they help Draw pictures of people visited Dramatic play	*School Helpers* Elaine Hoffman and Jane Hefflefinger Melmont Publishers, Inc. Chicago, 1955
D. Rules 1. firedrills 2. playground 3. halls	D. Have dry runs on fire drill procedure walking in halls Explain use of equipment and demonstrate	adult volunteers come in to help with safe use of playground equipment*
E. Establish routine 1. morning exercises 2. definite work time 3. free playtime and cleanup	E. Teacher leads children through same established routine each day More capable children can help those less able	place for everything must be provided bulletin board with day's routine on it

---

* Volunteers are from National Council of Jewish Women. Chart for helpers is put up in Massapequa. Appropriate service agencies can be contacted in your area.

TABLE 8 (*Continued*)
SOCIAL STUDIES

Units	Activities	Materials
4. group activities		
5. individual activities		
6. snack and recess time		
II. The Family		
A. Roles and relationships	A. Show and tell	photographs of children and their families
1. who are in family?	Role playing	pictures in magazines of family group and activities
2. how many?		playhouse equipment
3. pets?		hand puppets of family
		The Little Family
B. Work and help	B. Puppets	Lois Lenski
1. what do Mothers do?	Draw pictures of family	Doubleday and Co., Inc.
2. what do Fathers do?		New York, 1932
a. occupations		*Family Helpers*
b. at home		Elaine Hoffman and Jane Hefflefinger
3. how children can help?		Melmont Publishers, Inc.
		Chicago, 1952
C. Play	Bulletin board (making one with	Records: "Daddy Comes Home"
1. with brothers and sisters	the group)	"Let's Help Mommy"
2. recreation of whole family group	Listening to stories and singing	filmstrips
	songs	magazine pictures of furniture, houses, etc.
III. Home and Neighborhood	III. Take walk around school to see	
A. What kind of home do we live in?	school neighborhood	
B. Rooms of house	Have children bring snapshots of	
C. Neighbors	their homes	
1. respect for others' belongings	Cut out houses and learn addresses	
2. how they help us	Outline house on bulletin board;	
	fill rooms with pictures of what	
	belongs	

TABLE 8 (*Continued*)
SOCIAL STUDIES

Units	Activities	Materials
IV. Community Helpers	IV. Visit firehouse, library, post office, etc.	"My Kindergraph Kit"
A. Policeman, fireman, mailman		Follett Publishing Company
B. Doctor, dentist, nurse	Recommend parents take children on trips (school can't)	Chicago, Illinois
C. Grocer, milkman, etc.	Role playing	hand puppets
	Games ("Stop and Go")	traffic signs
	Puppets	Records: "I Want to be a ———"
		"The Men Who Come to Our House"
V. Holidays	V. Trace and cut out patterns of holiday symbols	*Some Days to Remember*
A. With historical significance		Alma Kehoe Reck & Helen Hall
1. Columbus Day	Color pictures of holiday stories	Fitcher
2. Veteran's Day	Make craft objects depicting holidays	Melmont Publishing, Inc.
3. Thanksgiving		Chicago, 1958
4. Washington's and Lincoln's Birthdays	Read stories about holidays and events	library books
5. Memorial Day	Learn songs	record: "Come to the Party"
6. Flag Day	Dramatic play	
	Participation in school or community programs	
B. Fun days (for children)		
1. Halloween		
2. Christmas		
3. Valentine's Day		
4. Easter		

TEACHER REFERENCES

A Guide or Kindergarten Teachers. Massapequa Public Schools, 1958.

Connor, Frances P. and Talbot, Mabel E.: An experimental Curriculum for Young Mentally Retarded Children. Bureau of Publications, Teachers College, Columbia University, New York, 1964.

Carlson, Bernice Wells and Ginglend, David R.: *Play Activities for the Retarded Child.* Abingdon, New York, 1961.

Cruiekshank, William M. and others: *A Teaching Method for Brain-Injured and Hyperactive Children.* Syracuse, 1961.

Wallace, J. E.: *Education of Mentally Handicapped Children.* Wallin, Harper, New York, 1955.

Kirk, Samuel, and Johnson, G. Orville: *Educating the Retarded Child.* Houghton Mifflin Co., Cambridge, Mass. 1951.

Chapter 3

The Intermediate Level Class for the Educable Retardate

LEON BARSKY

PHILOSOPHY AND GOALS

EDUCATION and society are so intertwined that it is difficult to separate one from the other. The educational process is the instrument through which a society seeks to implement the ideals by which it lives. In essence, education is the mirror of a living culture. If the educational goals are examined, one can see reflected the philosophy of that society. Democratic society recognizes differences in its population and attempts to provide experiences from which all may benefit. Accepting this premise, this chapter concerns itself with a program for elementary (intermediate) retarded children, which offers the most meaningful and enriching experiences possible for *each child*. Such education necessitates a profound respect for individual differences and recognizes that not all will benefit equally from the same curriculum.

In our culture, the goals of education for mentally retarded children may be broadly categorized as including the following:

1. *self-development* with opportunities for self-expression, for physical growth and health, for safety and survival, and for meeting crises with stability and serenity;

2. *interpersonal and intergroup relations* through sound growth as a citizen of the world around them;

3. *understanding of people and things* in the world he knows, with interrelationships to his personal life and to the life of his community;

4. *use of essential skills* of oral communication, listening, read-

ing, writing, arithmetic, and spelling to the extent that he can understand and profit from them.

OBJECTIVES AND GUIDELINES

One of the first steps in the development and implementation of a curriculum is to set forth a series of statements which serve as guidelines for direction and purpose. These guiding principles include the following:

1. The curriculum should provide for all the learning experiences in which children should participate under the school's direction.
2. The curriculum should present those learnings which are based upon the needs and interests of children with limited abilities.
3. The major objectives of a curriculum for retarded children are essentially the same as for all children; the differences will be in degree and varieties of application.
4. The curriculum should be fashioned in such a manner as to allow for considerable freedom on the part of the teacher and the pupils to determine the immediate goals and the best methods for achieving these goals.
5. The curriculum should provide the teacher with a variety of suggested methods and materials to assist in attaining the goals that were set forth.
6. Curriculum planning should be an ongoing process and curriculum materials should be prepared to allow for easy revision.
7. Curriculum construction should have as its aim not only the preparation of materials but, equally important, the growth of the teacher in the art of teaching.
8. Large-scale participation by teachers, administrators, parents, pupils, and consultants should always be a major goal.

Although these aforementioned objectives appear exceedingly simple, they are in fact quite complex and far-reaching. If the general guiding principles of the curriculum are effectively developed, they should answer the following questions:

1. Are the child's physical, mental, and emotional needs being met?

2. Can the child get along with others while understanding himself?
3. Has he learned to travel and move about safely?
4. Has he learned to enjoy life and use leisure time effectively?
5. Has he learned how to earn a living and successfully manage his finances?
6. Can he talk and use symbols in his culture to the degree that he communicates and interacts well with his fellow man?

Although this curriculum, as presented throughout the chapter, can be a valuable adjunct in the teaching process, it can not be seen as operating in a vacuum; it must be combined with a basic philosophy—content, while important, is correlative to intelligent, imaginative, and creative presentation.

The retarded child, like most children, is a "copy cat." He likes to do what others are doing. He likes to feel he is "normal" and one of the "gang." It is encumbent upon the special class teacher to meet this need, while at the same time always being aware that reality does exist and that the child with his limitations can not be expected to produce what in the final analysis is beyond him. Thus, while the mentally retarded child *can* be original, his very originality will be elementary in nature and limited in amount and scope.

Because education for all children is in the throes of technological upheaval, new methods and more sophisticated techniques must be employed by the special class teacher. The teacher will need to be aware of the variety of materials and resources available. It is with this in mind that this chapter deals with suggestions of various activities, materials, and techniques to aid in creating a more effective and meaningful environment.

AUDIOVISUAL INSTRUCTIONAL MATERIALS

The chalkboard traditionally is always available for immediate use. However, the use of the overhead projector, with teacher-made transparencies, commercially-prepared transparencies, and transparencies that the children have participated in producing are very effective for creating sound learning experiences. Charts, both teacher-made and commercial, as well as flat pictures and posters, are often helpful as display and bulletin boards. This chapter suggests the use of films and filmstrips, tapes, phonograph records, radio and television programs, models, dioramas, slides, 8mm single concept films, opaque projectors, and other special materials.

Community visits and field trips should be used to enrich learning situations. A tour through the neighborhood or a particular destination in the community is a good beginning. More elaborate trips will be appropriate in relation to specific objectives. Participation in planning learning to answer questions from observations, and exercising acceptable social behavior are skills which can be developed.

In some schools, a classified list of potentially helpful resource people is kept on file. Parents, adult friends of the children, members of the faculty, as well as professionals in the community, may be willing to visit your classroom and speak to the class.

As stated earlier, a variety of instructional techniques may be employed, but the resourcefulness and ingenuity in the selection and presentation of material rests always in the hands of the teacher.

CURRICULUM FOR INTERMEDIATE RETARDATES
(I.Q.: 50-75; Chronological Age: 9-13)

The curriculum for the intermediate class is an extension of the curriculum outlined for the primary class. The same general objectives are applicable to this age group; the difference exists in terms of degree.

Many children entering the intermediate class at the age of nine or ten will be unable to read or will be reading at the beginning first grade level. When the children leave the intermediate class at the age of thirteen or fourteen, they should have developed sufficient skills in the basic tool subjects to enable them to adjust to the program of the secondary school special class.

In developing a curriculum for the intermediate class, it is necessary that a well-balanced program be developed which will include tool subjects and areas of experience. Fundamental skills must be taught in a meaningful way to each child through the use of activities, real life situations, units of experience, and audiovisual aids in order to bring the concepts to the child so he can see, feel, and experience them.

The inclusion of the tool subjects makes the curriculum of such a special class not totally different from that of a regular elementary class. The tool subjects, however, should not be considered a separate entity but should be treated as part of the total learning experience related to the child and his immediate environment.

The informational content of the curriculum for the intermediate class is encompassed in the "areas of living" approach. This approach is best suited to meet the educational, vocational, and social needs of the pupils. In keeping with the format of the preceeding chapter, the "areas of living" are broken down into units and subunits with suggested and recommended materials. Some of the activities, particularly those dealing with language, numbers, and manual skills, because of the scarcity of instructional materials available within the interest and achievement level of these children, have to be developed by the special education teacher.

There are various methods and techniques that may be utilized for the implementation of the curriculum for the intermediate class: the unit approach, the experimental approach, and the traditional subject matter approach.

The unit approach provides the child with a concrete type of subject matter which is centered around his immediate surroundings and needs. The unit for these children should be short in deference to their limited attention span.

The experimental approach provides more life-like experiences focusing upon activities rather than formal, lecture-type presentation. These experiences should include field trips, dramatization in the classroom, guest speakers, and participation by the children in any project which relates to their life experiences.

The traditional subject matter approach concerns itself primarily with the teaching of the tool subjects of reading, writing, spelling, and arithmetic. It should provide the child with information which is within his comprehension while related to his life experiences. Repetition, with the use of interesting and diversified materials and presentations, is vital to these children.

Areas of Study

The curriculum may be divided into the following areas of study:

AREA I Social Studies
I. The Home
II. Transportation
III. Holidays and Seasons
IV. America the Beautiful

AREA II Health and Hygiene
I. Personal Health
II. Recreation
III. Safety

AREA III Language Arts
I. Reading
II. Oral Communications
III. Spelling and Handwriting

AREA IV Arithmetic
I. Computation Skills
II. Arithmetic Understanding in Everyday Living

AREA V Science
I. Things That Live in Our World
II. Weather, Climate, Seasons, Temperature
III. The Universe

AREA I—SOCIAL STUDIES

Curriculum content in social studies is planned sequentially to meet the needs of each pupil in relation to his understanding of (1) his home and school; (2) his place in the home, school, and neighborhood; (3) a broader view of neighborhood facilities; (4) the ways of living in the community; and (5) the ways of living in both the city and the country.

The potentialities for mental development will differ among the various members of a class. Some children will be restricted mentally to a limited understanding of the immediate neighborhood while others may learn to understand and cope with concrete experiences relating to a city or even a national area. Much of a child's ability to understand various concepts will depend upon the socioeconomic level and culture of his family background. In a family where a child travels to various parts of the country with his mother and father, there will be personal experiences from which he may build concepts of distance. Such a concept cannot adequately be mastered by the mentally retarded child who never leaves his immediate neighborhood.

A program of social studies which involves the child's total curriculum should be based upon concrete experiences which will help the child to develop a healthy personality and reach as high a level of educational achievement as possible. Skills and work habits should be used and practiced within the environment the child knows best until he becomes a self-sustaining citizen.

To provide for optimal growth, a mentally retarded child needs meaningful experiences which move gradually from the known to the unknown.

TABLE 9
SOCIAL STUDIES

Unit	Activities	Materials
I. Homes		16mm Films
A. Types of houses	Bring in photos of their homes or draw pictures of their homes	*New House—Where It Comes From* (Coronet)
B. Steps in building a house	Walk around neighborhood and view different types of homes	*Shelter* (EBF)
C. People who make our homes	Visit houses under construction	*Building a House* (EBF)
D. Materials needed	Discussion of how to plan a house	*Lumber for Houses* (EBF)
E. How homes are heated	Have children bring in scraps of construction materials	*Jimmy Visits the City* (Coronet)
F. Appliances in the home	Make scrapbooks of different types of homes	Filmstrips
G. Additional home comforts	List different jobs involved in building a house	*Houses* (EBF)
H. Living with others in harmony	Class project of construction of diarama depicting the community	*Kinds of Houses* (EBF)
I. Responsibility in the home	Make a map of the community showing location of various community resources (police station, fire dept., etc.)	*Men Who Build Houses* (EBF)
J. Manners and courtesy at home	List different fuels for home heating	*Tools and Materials for Building Houses* (EBF)
1. sharing	Discuss value of ability to make simple home repairs	*Why We Need Houses* (EBF)
2. helping	Discussion of home tasks, chores, and duties	*How We Get Our Homes Series* (S.V.E.)
3. pleasant manners	Discuss appearance of home and care of surroundings	Books
4. not being loud	Collect pictures, make scrapbooks, posters of various home appliances	*True Book of Houses* (Childrens Press)
5. telephone courtesy		*To Watch A Building Go Up* (Putnam & Sons)
		Everybody Has a House (Scott Inc.)
		Project Boy—Lenski, L. (Lippincott Co.)
		How We Get Our Shelter (Benefic Press)

TABLE 9 (*Continued*)
SOCIAL STUDIES

Unit	Activities	Materials
	List those appliances which are essential, those which are luxury items	*How A House is Built*—Benenson (Criterion Books)
	Learn and practice housekeeping activities which can be carried over into the home (cooking, sewing, cleaning)	*Other Materials*
	Discuss family members and their responsibilities to each other (helping mother and father, taking care of baby sisters and brothers, doing things for grandparents, being quiet when someone is ill, remembering birthdays, sending thank you notes for presents, etc.)	magazines and newspapers
		craft materials (wood, clay, glue, paint, etc.)
		materials
	Read stories about cooperation in home activities composed by class	telephone company sends demonstration phones and booklets for classroom use
II. Transportation		*16mm Films*
A. How we travel	Visit automobile agency or garage	*The Big Wide Highway* (Coronet)
B. Coming to school	Discuss and list ways how public transportation helps make our daily life easier	*Building A Highway* (EBF)
		The Bus Driver (EBF)
C. Travel for pleasure	Construct diorama or model car garage public transportation facility (airport, bus, and train station)	*Safety On The Way To School* (Coronet)
		Boats (EBF)
		The Freight Train (EBF)
		Airplane Trip (EBF)
		The Passenger Train (EBF)
		Transportation By Air (McGraw-Hill)

TABLE 9 *(Continued)*
SOCIAL STUDIES

Unit	Activities	Materials
D. Types of transportation	If possible have children assemble model cars and planes from kits—either in committee or as individual projects	*Transportation In The Modern World* (Coronet)
1. automobiles	Display map or street guide of the community	*Truck Driver* (EBF)
2. trains and railroads	Display sample street signs and traffic signs	*Trucks That Serve Our City* (Tomkins)
3. trucks and buses	Discuss modes of travel (auto, school bus, public bus, taxi, trains, airplane)	*Big Trains Rolling* (American Association of Railroads)
4. airplanes and airports	Write and list familiar landmarks on way to school	*The Busy Harbor* (Coronet)
5. boats and ships	Science activity in finding direction (east, west, south, north)	*Airplane Trip By Jet* (EBF)
	Make and display signs or posters of direction and safety traffic signs	*Airport* (EBF)
	Have school bus driver visit class	*Fred and Billy Take An Airplane Trip* (Coronet)
	Make posters illustrating different modes of transportation	*Harbor Pilot* (Baily)
	Display travel posters from travel agency	*FILMSTRIPS*
	Read books about different means of travel (see materials)	*Travel is Fun—Part I and II* (McGraw Hill)
	Show films and filmstrips on transportation (see materials)	*People and Goods Travel* (Jim Handy)
	Visit public transportation and travel facilities	*Transportation In the Past* (EBF)
	Dramatize with play money paying fares and receiving change	*Safety On the Bicycle* (McGraw Hill)
		Buses (Jim Handy)
		Bus Driver (McGraw Hill)
		Highway Transportation (EBF)
		Safe and Sound Along The Way (SVE)
		School Bus Safety (McGraw Hill)
		Trucks (Jim Handy)
		Airports and Airplanes (SVE)
		Machines Help Us Travel (Eye Gate)

TABLE 9 (*Continued*)
SOCIAL STUDIES

Unit	Activities	Materials
	Invite parents or community individuals whose work is related to the transportation area	*Rail Transportation* (EBF)
	List ways in which transportation plays an important role in our daily living (food, clothing, recreation)	*Water Transportation* (EBF)
	Use math skills in determining distance (measurement) and duration (time) in traveling	*Travel In Space* (EBF)
	Compute cost of fare for different trips	BOOKS
	List transportation facilities in community	*Davy Goes Places*—Lenski (Walch Inc.)
	Collect pictures or make scrapbooks of different automobiles or other types of transportation	*How We Travel On Land* (Benefic Press)
	Write and spell words that are selected from unit of transportation	*How We Travel on Water* (Benefic Press)
	Discuss and write experience chart of students own travel experience	*Transportation* (Childrens Press)
	Construct large mural illustrating modes of travel and the development of travel from early days (can be dramatized as a television program)	*Big Book of Cars* (Grosset and Dunlap Inc.)
		Who Built The Highway (Melmont Co.)
		Trucks and Tractors and Trailors (Putman)
		Three Boys And A Train (Scribner and Sons)
		First Book of Airplanes (Watts Inc.)
		Trucks and Trucking (Putman and Sons)
		Freight Trains (Putman and Sons)
		How Airplanes Help Us (Benefic Press)
		Wonderful World of Transportation— Lee and Lambert (Garden City Books)
		True Book of Transportation—Wilde (Childrens Press)
		Transportation—Cahn (Fideler)

TABLE 9 *(Continued)*
SOCIAL STUDIES

Unit	Activities	Materials
III. Holidays and Seasons A. Fall	Bring in signs of the changing season (leaves, ripe fruits, etc.) Discuss length of season Learn names of months in the Fall Make calendars Sing songs of fall Discuss harvest time	*Down Come The Leaves*—Bancroft (Crowell & Co.) *Golden Song Book* (Golden Press) *Exploring the New World* (Follett) *Journeys Through the Americas* (Allyn & Bacon) *The American Heritage Series* (Dell)
B. Columbus Day	Draw Columbus' ships Construct papier-mâché models of ships Draw round world (globe work) Act out Columbus' plea to Queen Isabella for financing of trip Discuss how you would feel if you discovered America	*The First Book of Holidays*—Burnett (Watts) *Why Is It A Holiday?*—McGovern (Random House) *The First Book of Festivals*—Reck (Watts) *America Sings*—Carmer (Alfred Knopf) *American Folk Songs for Children*— Seeger (Doubleday)
C. Halloween	Visit pumpkin farm Make own Halloween costumes Write scary stories Discuss Halloween—fact or fiction goblins, witches, haunted houses Plan Halloween party Discuss and collect funds for the Unicef-sharing concept Carve jack-o-lanterns—plant seeds or roast and serve salted	*UNICEF and the World*—Speiser (John Day Co.) *Leaves*—Caulfield (Coward McCann Pub.) *The Fireside Book of Childrens Songs*— Winn, Miller, Alcorn (Simon & Schuster) craft materials of various types
D. Thanksgiving	Discuss landing of Mayflower at Plymouth Rock	*The True Book of Indians*— T. Martini (Childrens Press)

TABLE 9 (*Continued*)
SOCIAL STUDIES

Unit	Activities	Materials
	Draw and make models of Pilgrims and Mayflower	*The Big Book of Indians*—S. Fletcher (Grossett & Dunlap)
	Dramatize the first Thanksgiving	*The First Book of Indians*—P. Brewster (Franklin Watts, Inc.)
	Plan a Thanksgiving dinner	*Frontiers of America Series* (Childrens Press)
	Make cornbread, cranberry sauce, etc.	
	Plant corn	*The Book of Indian Crafts and Costumes* —Mason (Ronald Press)
	Make scrap book of animals and fish eaten by Pilgrims	*A Child's Calendar*—Updike (Alfred Knopf)
	Make displays of bows and arrows used by Indians	*Poems for Seasons and Celebrations*— Noyer (World Pub. Co.)
	Make Indian handcrafts	*How Animals Tell Time*—Selsam (Morrow Pub.)
	Learn Indian rhythms and dances (tom-toms)	*When Animals Change Clothes*—May (Holiday House)
	Construct tom-toms	
E. Winter	Discuss safety on ice	
	Discuss dressing warmly in cold weather	
	Draw pictures of winter fun	
	Sing songs of winter	
	Discuss animal hibernation, bird migration	
	Construct bird feeders to hang outdoors for nonmigratory birds	
	Make styrofoam or papier-mâché snowmen	

TABLE 9 (*Continued*)
SOCIAL STUDIES

Unit	Activities	Materials
F. Chanukah and Christmas (specific national traditions)	Sing songs of Christmas and Chanukah	*The Hanukkah Story*—Beal, M. (Behrman)
1. Mexican pinata	Make Mexican piñata	*Hanukkah*—Norma Simon (Crowell Co.)
2. Swedish	Plan Christmas party	*Holiday Handicraft*—Jordan (Harcourt Brace)
3. Jewish (Menorah)	Plan for grab bag (sharing)	*Frontiers of American History* (Fawcett Pub.)
	Read "Twas The Night Before Christmas"	
	Make cookies and candy	
	Make gifts for family	
	Trim a tree	
	Draw or construct menorahs, dreidls Santa Claus, candy canes, reindeer	
G. Lincoln's and Washington's Birthdays	Draw or construct log cabins	*Presidents of the United States* (Simon & Schuster)
	Make silhouettes of Lincoln	*Golden Book of American History* (Simon & Schuster)
	Discuss role of President then and now	*Birthdays*—Patterson, L. (Garrard Pub. Co.)
	Discuss Lincoln's boyhood, Washington's boyhood	Records: "Songs to Grow On—"Folkways"
	Discuss Civil War, Emancipation Proclamation	"Children Sing On Hanukkah"
H. Valentine's Day	Act out assassination of Lincoln	"Songs of the North and South" (Columbia)
	Draw northern and southern soldiers	*Green Is For Growing*—Lubell (Rand McNally)
	Locate major battle sites on maps	*America Travels*—Dagleish (MacMillan)
	Sing "Yankee Doodle"	*Safety Can Be Fun*—Leaf (Lippincott)
	Dramatize cherry tree incident	
	Draw Mt. Vernon	
I. Spring, Easter, and Passover	Draw maypoles, spring flowers, birds, etc.	
	Construct a maypole	

TABLE 9 (*Continued*)
SOCIAL STUDIES

Unit	Activities	Materials
	Dance around maypole	Red Cross *First Aid Book*: Health,
	Sing songs of spring	Safety, Chpts. I-IV (MacMillan Co.)
	Discuss length of season	send for travel posters—airlines, steam-
	Plant seeds, watch germination	ship companies, chambers of com-
	Hatch baby chicks in incubator	merce, etc.
	Color Easter eggs	
	Have jellybean hunt	
	Discuss Passover	
J. Summer	Describe vacation fun	
	Discuss vacation safety (swimming rules, etc.)	
	Bring in travel posters, vacationland folders	
	Demonstrate artificial respiration, first-aid	
	Write letters for travel information	
	Discuss plans for summer camp	
IV. America the Beautiful	Indicate broad geographical areas of the United States	*In All Our States* (Scott Foresman)
The North	Locate specific mountains, oceans	*Our Hemisphere* (American Book Co.)
The South	Bring in pictures of different types of terrain	*The Changing New World* (Silver Burdett)
The East		
The West		
The 49th and 50th States		
Climate Changes		
Mountains, Rivers, Oceans		

AREA II—HEALTH AND HYGIENE

The area of health and hygiene includes instruction in personal care, recreation, community hygiene, social and emotional adjustment, and safety. Health knowledge and habits can be realized through learning how to care for the body. Recreation has many goals; improving bodily health, constructive use of leisure time, creating opportunities for exercising such character traits as fair play, self-control, and good sportsmanship.

Community health can be seen as a civic responsibility as well as acquisition of knowledge of the services offered by the community. Social and emotional adjustment is aided by helping the children recognize life problems. Safety in the school, on the street, and in the home is improved through the teaching of accident prevention.

TABLE 10
HEALTH AND HYGIENE

Units	Activities	Materials
I. Personal Health	Make displays of different fabrics:	*16MM films*
A. Personal appearance	1. collect pictures for scrapbooks, illustrating combinations of clothing according to the season, occasion and style	*Where Does Our Food Come From* (Coronet)
1. Where we get our clothing		*Where Does Our Meat Come From* (Coronet)
2. What materials clothes are made of	2. display catalogues to illustrate articles according to price	*Truck Farmer* (EBF)
3. Clothes for different types of activity	Collect swatches of fabrics and illustrate procedures for care and conservation	*Bread—Milk—Eggs* (EBF)
		Dairy Farm (Coronet)
		Food Store (EBF)
4. Clothes for different seasons	Discussion of merchandise—quality and value	*Behind the Scenes at the Supermarket* (Film Associates)
5. Buying clothes	Relationship between value and cost	*Foods From Grains* (Coronet)
6. Care of clothes	Develop concept of sales specials and their advantages and disadvantages	*Filmstrips*
		The Bakery (EBF)
	Read and discuss catalogs and ads relating to purchase of clothing	*Food Store* (EBF)
		Story of Foods Series (SVE)
	Compute cost of clothing	*Getting Food Ready for Market* (EBF)
	Math concepts of measurement and money (making change with bills and coins)	*The Grocer* (McGraw-Hill)
		How We Get Our Food (SVE)
		BOOKS
	Sewing projects	*How We Get Our Dairy Food* (Benefic Press)
	Visit community stores (dept. stores) that sell clothing	*Let's Go to a Supermarket* (Putnam & Sons)
	Discuss informally their own articles of clothing	*How Foods are Preserved* (Benefic Press)
	Introduce concepts of raw materials	*The First Book of Food* (Watts Inc.)

TABLE 10 (*Continued*)
HEALTH AND HYGIENE

Units	Activities	Materials
	Make chart of "My Clothing." Have class identify articles—what they are made of where it comes from (plant, animal, man-made, etc.)	*Books* *Bill's Story of the Wholesale Produce Market* (Scribner & Sons)
	Pictures cut from magazines may be projected with opaque projector	*Your Food and You* (Morrow & Co.)
	Introduce concept of assembly line production	*Your Breakfast and the People Who Make It* (Doubleday)
	Have children work on weaving projects	*The Frozen Foods Plant* (Childrens Press)
	Show films and filmstrips on clothing	*First Book of Supermarkets* (Watts, Inc.)
	Have parents of children (when possible) who work in clothing factories come in and speak to the class	*Let's Go to a Bakery* (Putnam & Son)
	Discuss why personal appearance is so important; making friends, getting a job, etc.	*Nothing To Eat But Food*—Jupo (Dutton Co.)
		Nothing To Wear But Clothes—Jupo (Dutton Co.)
B. Personal hygiene and cleanliness	Teach proper care of teeth (brush, curb intake of sweets, visits to dentist)	*Scientific Living Series* (The How and Why Books) (Singer Co.)
	Discuss bathing	
	Discuss hair care	bring in large-scale models of teeth and toothbrushes for demonstration
	Visit dentist, clinics, hospitals	
	Discuss complexion care	write for material on Presidential Program for Physical Fitness

TABLE 10 (*Continued*)
HEALTH AND HYGIENE

Units	Activities	Materials
C. Play, rest, and exercise	Discuss and play games for better health	get charts and pamphlets from drug and food companies
	Discuss value of rest after exercise	get models of heart, eye, ear, etc.
	Discuss value of exercise for body	use models of "visible Man" and "Visible Woman"
	Discuss muscle building	*Your Wonderful Teeth*—Schloat (Scribners & Sons)
	Stress good sleeping habits	
D. Food and nutrition	Show films on good eating habits, food, nutrition, cleanliness	
1. How we get our food	Make posters on basic foods	
2. Transportation of food	Discuss food as source of energy (fuel)	
3. Food stores	Read basic food charts	
4. People who work in food stores	Keep daily log of food intake	
5. Seven basic foods for well balanced diet	Sources of food and how they get to us	
6. Places to eat (types of restaurants	Compute cost of food for a meal	
	Group cooperation in planning a menu and preparing simple meals for visitors	
	Food combinations—typical breakfast, lunch, dinner	
	Collect and make scrapbook of different foods of the "basic seven"	
	Make class mural to illustrate source of various basic foods	
	Read menus from restaurants, plan selections for various meals, and compute cost	
	Field trips to local bakery, commercial bakery, other food processing sources	

TABLE 10 *(Continued)*
HEALTH AND HYGIENE

Units	Activities	Materials
	List rules for good health based on good eating habits	
	Discuss how the body uses food	
	Discuss what is needed to make food grow	
	Visit local farm, cannery, etc.	
	Learn to write and spell names of common foods	
	Compute cost of school lunches in cafeteria	
	Compute family food budget using newspaper ads	
	Discuss social behavior and customs typical of public dining places	
	Class skit dramatizing visit to restaurant	
	Possible placement of class members in school cafeteria as workers, busboys, waitresses, helpers	
	Show films on growing and processing of school	
	List occupations involved in processing food from source to table	

TABLE 10 (Continued)
HEALTH AND HYGIENE

Units	Activities	Materials
II. Recreation	Discuss ways of making good use of leisure time	*16mm Films* *Fun On the Playground* (EBF)
A. Places to play	Discuss and list places the neighborhood and community provides for children and grownups to have fun	*Let's Go To The Circus* (EBF) *SoftBall For Boys* (Coronet)
B. How to play	Discuss and list types of equipment usually found in these facilities	*I'm No Fool Having Fun* (Disney Productions)
C. How to choose and enjoy friends	Draw or cut pictures of different recreation activities	*We Explore The Beach* (Coronet) *We Explore The Woodland* (Coronet) *Winter Wonderland* (United World Govt.)
	Discuss advantages of indoor and outdoor recreational facilities	*Good Sportsmanship* (Coronet)
	List recreation activities best suited for different types of weather conditions	*Better Use of Leisure Time* (Coronet) *Fun That Builds Good Health* (Coronet)
	Develop and discuss rules for proper use of recreation facilities (behavior, manners, etc.)	*Fun Of Making Friends* (Coronet)
	Have children report on their own recreational experience—develop reading activity from these experiences	*Filmstrips* *Fall Fun* (Eye Gate) *Family Fun* (EBF) *Going To School Is Fun* (Eye Gate)
	Dramatize typical situation and discuss proper attitude of fair play, etc.	*Having Fun In A City* (Eye Gate) *Neighborhood Picnic* (SVE) *Our Parks and Playgrounds* (EBF)
	Have each child name his favorite sport or recreational activity—write and read story about this activity	*Spring Fun* (Eye Gate) *Summer Fun* (Eye Gate) *Winter Fun* (Eye Gate) *Travel Is Fun* (McGraw Hill)
	Have children dramatize or perform a charade on a recreation activity—have	*We Take A Trip Series* (McGraw Hill)

TABLE 10 (*Continued*)
HEALTH AND HYGIENE

Units	Activities	Materials
	the other children try to guess what it is	*Books*
	Show films and filmstrips on recreation and play (see materials).	*The Buttons and the Boy Scouts* (Benefic Press)
	List types of hobbies or activities and games that can be done at home	*The Buttons Go Camping* (Benefic Press)
	Develop a time for recreation or play and for home and school responsibilities	*Playground Fun* (Children's Press)
	Make simple games for home such as checkerboard, bean bag, etc.	*Good Times at The Circus* (Melmont Pub.)
	Develop interest in using a camera display photographs	*Games For Boys and Girls* (Abingdon Press)
	Read *T.V. Guide* and discuss favorite programs	*Bingo Books* (Row Peterson)
	Develop interest in social dancing and listening to records (popular—classical)	*As Others Like You* (McKnight Pub. Co.)
	List rules for care of equipment and furniture at home and when at play	*Good Times Together* (Lyons & Carnahan)
	Discuss fairness with other members at home in sharing T.V.—respect of privacy, etc.	*Magazines*
	Discuss and list reasons for inviting a friend home	*Playmates*
	List reasons for not inviting someone to your home	*Boys' Life*
		Children's Activities
		Highlights

TABLE 10 (*Continued*)
HEALTH AND HYGIENE

Units	Activities	Materials
III. *Safety* A. On the street B. In school C. On the playground D. At home E. Safety signs F. People who work for safety	Have school crossing guard or policeman speak to the class on safety in streets Have various posters displayed on safety in the streets (bikes, etc.) Construct traffic sign, danger signs, etc. Have children find pictures in newspapers and magazines illustrating results of poor safety habits that create accidents Find pictures about preventing accidents at home, school, playground, streets, at work, shopping, traveling Visit local fire station, first-aid or ambulance service, hospital, etc. List and review school rules for safety in school and on playground Show films and filmstrips on safety (see materials) Read pamphlets and books on safety (see materials) Discuss and list how to prevent accidents List and draw posters of community helpers related to safety and prevention of accidents Draw pictures illustrating safety practices	*16mm Films* *The Fireman* (EBF) *Health In Our Community* (EBF) *The Policeman* (EBF) *Your Friend The Doctor* (EBF) *The Nurse* (EBF) *Safe Living In Your Community* (Coronet) *School Rules: How They Help Us* (Coronet) *Your Health In The Community* (Coronet) *First Aid Fundamentals* (Coronet) *On Two Wheels* (Jam Handy) *Safety On The Way To School* (Coronet) *Safety To And From School* (Young America Film) *Rules and Laws* (EBF) *Filmstrips* *Fire Department* (McGraw Hill) *Our Fire Department* (EBF) *Our Police Department* (EBF) *Policeman* (EBF) *Policeman and Fireman* (SVE)

TABLE 10 (*Continued*)
HEALTH AND HYGIENE

Units	Activities	Materials
	Discuss and read about first-aid procedures	*We Make Some Safety Rules* (McGraw Hill)
	Discuss what to do in case of accidents	*You And Safety* (Filmstrip House)
	Discuss fire drill and air raid drill in school	**Books**
	Make chart illustrating fire and accident hazards	*Fireman Fred* (Whitman)
	Read and spell words related to safety topics (i.e. "danger," "poison," "caution," etc.)	*Policeman Paul* (Whitman)
	Invite school nurse to demonstrate first aid	*Let's Take A Trip To A Fire House* (Putnam's Sons)
	Create (mock) first-aid stations within classroom	*To A Hospital* (Putnam's Sons)
		Mr. Ferguson Of The Fire Department (Whittlesey House)
		True Book of Policemen and Firemen (Childrens Press)
		Let's Go To A Police Station (Putnam's Sons)
		Doctor John (Melmont Pub.)
		How Hospitals Help Us (Benefic Press)

AREA III—LANGUAGE ARTS

The language arts portion of the curriculum interlocks reading, oral communication, spelling and handwriting, and written expression. Considering the wide range of individual differences of children in the special class, it is impossible to follow a predetermined plan without finding it necessary to make frequent changes. There is a tailor-made quality to this facet of the program.

The core of the language arts program is reading. While regular basic readers can be used, they can serve two purposes: they can provide moments of reading for pleasure and leisure time; they can serve as guides for providing information. Additionally, considerable time can be spent in helping the children learn to read for their protection and safety.

Some pupils will be capable of learning to read simple materials dealing with basic information. Some will be able to acquire sufficient skill to read more than the simplest materials written for pure appreciation and enjoyment. Some instruction on how to look at pictures in books and magazines for information and enjoyment should be included in the educational activities of a particular unit.

A variety of instructional techniques will need to be employed by the teacher, and many types of reading materials will need to be used in the classroom if each child is to progress to the maximum of his ability. Because of the scarcity of reading materials geared to these children's needs, interests, and abilities, the teacher must be resourceful in selecting, adapting, and preparing instructional materials. Commercially-prepared textbooks can be used for a portion of the reading program. Experience stories, graded newspapers, signs, labels, magazines, and prepared transparencies (for overhead projection) have been found to be valuable in developing reading skills. There is an advantage in using some teacher-prepared material to meet specific needs; colorful transparencies may be created by the teacher and students.

Children may make individual booklets or picture dictionaries of words, phrases, and sentences. These may be illustrated by using the child's own drawings or cut out pictures. Audiovisual material may be used to build up an experiential background for reading, to stimulate a desire to read, to give meaning to reading activities, and to test knowledge of what has been read.

Reading

In implementing the reading program, certain basic concepts should be understood by the teacher. These include the following:

1. knowing the mental age of the child;
2. being aware of the present achievement level of each child;
3. choosing materials appropriate to his social interests;
4. being prepared to give the child step by step assistance in phonics, in the use of contextual clues, and in individual reading guidance;
5. knowing how to group children for reading so that the optimal learning climate can be effected;
6. realizing the importance of instilling confidence in the child's own estimation of his ability;
7. encouraging the use of a wide variety of reading material for independent activities.

A Further Note on Grouping

Grouping of children for reading activities is a device which will help the mentally retarded child in acquiring interest and skills in reading. Such grouping should be tentative and flexible and the childs' needs and interests should govern how long he remains with a particular group. Sometimes he may work with more than one group in reading. There are various purposes which will dictate the type of groups to be formed. Children on the same instructional level may be grouped together for basic instruction or for having some special reading need, such as gaining more skills in word recognition; special interest groups can also be formed. The number of groups depends upon many factors including the range of abilities and the variety of needs and interests. The size of the groups is also dependent upon the above mentioned factors. It is essential that individual reading be done with the teacher whenever possible.

Oral Communications

The child is constantly utilizing a variety of communication skills as he uses his kinesthetic, olfactory, gustatory, auditory, and visual senses. He is constantly exploring his home, his school, and his community. It is incumbent upon the school to help the child learn to express himself orally and to communicate by appropriate signs, symbols, and body postures what his needs are. Additionally, we would expect him to adequately interpret what those around him are trying to say. He has to learn that communication is an interaction between him and the world. To facilitate this interaction we utilize a variety of tools and techniques. For example, there is much free conversation between teacher and pupils, parents and children. The child needs to hear language to become familiar with it and use it. Each day he hears new experience stories and has old ones repeated. He learns to repeat happenings, poems, and "home-made" songs.

Spelling and Handwriting

When the child is ready, regular brief, supervised practice in handwriting becomes a part of the program. All children should learn to recognize and then to write their names. All should recognize and most will learn to write and to spell their parents' names. If the transition to cursive writing is too difficult, children should be allowed to use manuscript writing for all purposes, because sometimes mentally retarded children will never be called on to use cursive writing. Many will learn to recognize and use sentences, use capitals at the beginning of all names and sentences, write friendly letters, business letters, notes, invitations, grocery lists, simple stories, and fill out blanks.

Spelling words are taught in connection with the words a child needs in everyday living. As new experiences stimulate the need, many words will be learned. Here too methodical practice will be needed before the correct spelling of some of the words becomes automatic.

TABLE 11
LANGUAGE ARTS

Units	Activities	Materials
I. Reading **A. Developing skills** 1. development of listening and comprehension 2. visual and auditory discrimination 3. left to right sequence 4. sequence of ideas 5. development of word attack 6. development of word recognition 7. development of sight vocabulary 8. development of background information **B. Applying reading skills** 1. reading signs, labels, charts 2. reading developmental reading series 3. competency in simple dictionary skills 4. reading child's own address, using phone directory 5. reading magazines and catalogues 6. reading for factual information 7. reading for enjoyment 8. appreciation and writing of poetry	Story time and poetry time Teacher reads to class Listening to records for sounds Listening for sounds around us (birds, planes, construction, sounds in school) Distinguishing between sounds (high—low, loud—soft, melodious—cacophonous, individual sounds—sound blends) Choral speaking A picture is cut into puzzle-like pieces; children asked to reassemble parts to form whole Phonic charts Children make sounds—class identifies Flash cards Lotto games Spelling bees Children bring in familiar objects to have class identify (tools, kitchen utensils, etc.) Children compose simple jingles, then illustrate for display Make picture dictionaries, scrapbooks, logs, experience charts	*All In A Day* (American Book Co.) *High On a Hill* (Row Peterson) *Up the Street and Down* (American Book Co.) *Around Green Hills* (American Book Co.) *Stories From Everywhere* (Lyons & Carnaham) *From All Around* (Bobbs-Merrill) *Book of Children's Poems* (Robt. L. Stevenson) Flash Cards Kenworthy Education Service Dr. Seuss Books (Houghton-Mifflin) Magazines: *Highlights, Childrens' Digest, Boys' Life* *Basic Vocabulary Series*—Dolch, E. W. (Garrard Press) *The Sport Readers*—Frissell and Freebele (MacMillan) *Practice Readers*—Grover and Stone (Webster) *Core Vocabulary Readers*—Huber (MacMillan) *Better Reading Books' Reading Labs* (Science Research Associates)

TABLE 11 (*Continued*)
LANGUAGE ARTS

Units	Activities	Materials
9. interpreting a story (audio and visual)	Chalkboard activities	*Driving the Reading Road*—Spencer (Lyons and Carnahan)
10. noting details and perceiving relationships (age, time, manner, space, number)	Make and label collections (leaves, rocks, shells, etc.) Dramatize stories; socio-drama, role playing, illustrate reading charts	*Eye and Ear Fun*—Stone (Webster) *Readers' Digest Reading Skill Builder* (Readers Digest ed. service)
11. interpreting figurative, descriptive and picturesque language	Develop a background of experience through field trips	*All About Series* (Random House) *Aviation Series* (MacMillan)
12. current events—learn to read newspaper	Learn to read transportation schedules, timetables, etc. Construction activities (dioramas, puppets, clay, woodwork, etc.) Read newspapers and periodicals headlines, local news, cartoons, weather reports, sports, ads, entertainment	*The Button Books* (Berkley-Cardy) *An Easy-to-read Book Series* (Mac-Millan) *The True Books* (Childrens Press) *Cowboy Sam Series* (Berkley-Cardy) *First Book Series* (Watts) *The Wonder Story Books* (Holt) *Little Wonder Books* (Merrill) *Reading For Fun* (Scott Foresman Co.)
II. *Oral Communication* A. How we send and receive messages 1. letters 2. telephone 3. radio 4. television 5. newspapers and magazines 6. movies	Make list of ways we communicate with our family and friends Make list of ways people farther away communicate with us Bring in local newspaper to class and discuss different types of messages (news, feature stories, classified ads, want ads) Show film and filmstrips on communication (see materials)	*Manners Can Be Fun*—Leaf (Lippincott) *Manners To Grow On*—Lee (Doubleday) *Adventures of a Letter*—Schloat (Scribners) *Marvels of the U.S. Mail*—Arnold (Abelard-Schuman) *The First Book of International Mail*—Hooke (Watts)

TABLE 11 (*Continued*)
LANGUAGE ARTS

Units	Activities	Materials
	Read supplementary books on communication (see materials)	*Any Mail For Me*—Jupo (Dodd, Mead & Co.)
	Contact local telephone representative for demonstration in proper use of the telephone	*All About Radio and Television*—Gould (Random House)
	Dramatize using the telephone for different situations	*Television Works Like This*—Bendick (McGraw Hill)
	List and read rules of proper use of the telephone	*What Makes TV Work*—Corbett (Little, Brown & Co.)
	Have class prepare their own telephone directory of friends and classmates	*Your Telephone and How it Works*—Schneider (McGraw Hill)
	Read directions for using telephone directory	*The Telephone*—Brinton (John Day Co.)
	Discuss rules for good listening	*The First Book of News*—Epstein (Watts)
	Plan trip to local newspaper office, post office, radio, or T.V. station (whenever possible)	*Let's Go to a Newspaper*—Bradley (Van Nostrand)
	Discuss favorite radio or T.V. program.	*Let's Take a Trip to a Newspaper*—Sootin (Putnam)
	Use of tape recorder in reading, spelling, or recording childrens reports	
	Develop and dramatize radio or T.V. program	
	List rule for effective written communication	
	Write letters to other classmates, friends or relatives	

TABLE 11 (*Continued*)
LANGUAGE ARTS

Units	Activities	Materials
	Utilize school audiovisual service for equipment dealing with the field of communication	*Individual Corrective English—Grades 1-6* (McCormick Mathers Co.)
	Make posters for bulletin board illustrating the development of communications and how it is used	Ditto Sheets (Continental Press)
	Discuss workers and occupations involved in providing different modes of communication	*The Practice Workbooks of English—1-6* (Treasure Books, Inc.)
	Review different methods used for sending and receiving messages, list materials and jobs for each	*English Is Our Language My Study Workbook, 1-4* (D.C. Heath & Co.)
		Basic Goals in Spelling I-IV Workbooks —Kottmeyer and Ware (Webster Pub. Co.)
III. Spelling and Handwriting	Spelling bees	*More Spelling I-IV* (Whitman Pub. Co.)
A. Writing sentences	Crossword puzzles (teacher made)	*Basic Keys I-IV* (J. P. Lippincott Co.)
B. Alphabetical order	Spelling bingo	*English, Your Language*—Wolfe and Dorsey (Allyn, Bacon & Co.)
C. Capital letters	Using the dictionary	*Good English #2* (Laidlaw Bros. Pub.)
D. Singular and plural	Using periodicals	
E. Opposites	Rhyming words	
F. Punctuation	Learn proper use of quotation marks	
G. Abbreviations	Learn abbreviations of months, days, of week, places, people	
H. Adjectives	Adding color to language	
	Writing thank you letter, invitations, etc.	

AREA IV—ARITHMETIC

A systematic program of arithmetic promotes the child's understanding, improves his retention, and helps him progress onward to new learnings. Meaning comes first then purposeful drill follows. It begins with the child's own number background. Experiences give him concepts and basic ideas. Number concepts are then related to the manipulation of numbers and to the computational skills.

Interestingly enough, retarded children have a better level of understanding of number concepts than would be expected in view of their characteristically weaker reading levels. Numbers, therefore, can be taught without a focus on high reading vocabulary. The logical easily illustrated and highly demonstrable qualities of arithmetic lend themselves very well to a sequential teaching process. The teacher, always aware of the common day-to-day applications of number facts, concepts, procedures, and manipulations, provides concrete teaching situations for the child. These can include totalling up shopping lists, understanding the handling of money, etc.

The scope of the arithmetic curriculum for mentally retarded pupils may be broadly classified into two categories:

I. Computational skills
   A. develop accuracy in operations with whole numbers and common fractions

II. Arithmetic understanding and use of numbers with meaning in everyday life
   A. develop meaningful conception of quantity
   B. develop meaningful arithmetic vocabulary
   C. develop understanding of essential arithmetical generalizations
   D. develop meanings in the fundamental arithmetical operations
   E. develop understanding of the meanings of measurements
   F. develop understanding of numerical comparisons, estimates, and approximations

G. develop ability to apply correctly arithmetical skills in in practical problems of everyday living [The mentally retarded are confronted daily with situations that involve the use of numbers. These situations call for ability to count, read and write numbers, measure, compute, understand vocabulary of quality, make numerical comparisons, estimates, and approximations, and apply these skills properly toward the solution of the problems.]

A variety of teaching techniques must be employed if these pupils are to be brought to their highest level of accomplishment in this areas. The basic step is that of developing readiness for each process of arithmetic as it is approached. The teacher must recognize that there is a logical sequence in arithmetic and that the pupil should be adequate in each level before undertaking the next. Since mentally retarded pupils learn slowly, it is obvious that they need considerable experience at each step before they are ready to proceed to the next. The arithmetic program for these pupils should not attempt to teach skills which are beyond the needs, interests, and abilities of the group.

TABLE 12
ARITHMETIC

Units	Activities	Materials
I. Computation Skills		*Filmstrips*
A. Numbers 1-100	Use of manipulative materials (chips, sticks, beads, blocks, checkers, pegs, dominoes, coins, etc.)	*Count to Find Out* (Eye Gate)
		Seeing Use of Numbers (Eye Gate)
B. Counting by 2's, 5's, 10's	Write numbers given orally	*Experience with Counting* (Eye Gate)
	Counting off on line	*Work and Play With No Series* (Eye Gate)
C. Applying number facts as suggested in first grade curriculum	Counting of objects in room, around school, etc.	*Putting Groups Together* (Eye Gate)
	Using abacus	*Taking a Group Apart* (Eye Gate)
D. Basic number facts through 20's	Using cuisenaire rods	*Addition and Subtraction Concepts* (Eye Gate)
E. Reading and writing addition and subtraction facts	Compute cost of food; conduct classroom store; use play money to make change	*The Game of How Many* (Eye Gate)
	Make up shopping lists	*The Basic Addition Table* (Colonial Films)
F. Readiness for multiplication and division—eventual problem solving	Make up problems about spending money	
G. Basic Roman numerals	Use of number line	*Films*
	Grouping of manipulative materials	*Addition for Beginners* (Coronet Films)
H. Money—subtraction, addition, making change	Collecting money for milk, Red Cross, PTA, etc.	*Arithmetic in the Food Store* (EBF)
	Buying lunch in school cafeteria	*Let's Count* (Coronet)
	Computing costs for class planned parties	*Books and Other Materials Working with Nos. 1-3* (Steck Co.)
		Living Arithmetic 3-4 (Ginn & Co.)
		Numbers at Work Books 1-4 (MacMillan Co.)
		Happy Times With Numbers (Allyn & Bacon)
		Three in One Book (workbook)

TABLE 12 (Continued)
ARITHMETIC

Units	Activities	Materials
		The Modern Mastery Drill in Arithmetic (Benton Review)
		Duplicating Materials (Continental Press)
		Numbers in Action (Scott Foresman)
		More About Numbers—Merton, Brueckner (Hold, Rhinehart, Winston)
		The Next Steps in Arithmetic I-II-III (Whitman Pub. Co.)
		cuisenaire rods
		abacus
		Addition Flash Cards Kenworthy Educational Service Ideal School Supply Co. Chicago, Ill.
		"Link Numbers" (Milton Bradley)
		"Number-ite The Judy Co. Minneapolis, Minn.
		GCMP—Greater Cleveland Math Program I-III
		SRA I-II (Science Research Associates)
		Pupils Fraction Kit Ideal School Supply Co. Chicago
		The Practice Workbook of Arithmetic— II-III (Treasure Books Inc.)

TABLE 12 (*Continued*)
ARITHMETIC

Units	Activities	Materials
		dominoes, checkers, bingo
		flannelboard
		Numbers—Old and New—Adler (H. W. Wilson Co.)
		Numbers Please—Andrews (Little Co.)
		Arithmetic Can Be Fun—Leaf (Lippincott)
II. Arithmetic Understanding		
A. Concepts:	Dances (right-left, up-down, etc.)	*The New Continental Practice Exercises —1-2* (Continental Press)
1. right—left	Make comparisons of age, size, height, weight, etc.	*Experimenting with Numbers*—Catherine Stern (Houghton Mifflin)
2. up—down	Putting things on shelves	*The First Book of Measurement*— Epstein (Watts)
3. in—out	Use money for coin size and value	*Learning To Think Series Red-Blue-Green Books* (S.R.A.)
4. high—low	Fractional experiences (half an apple, candy bar, etc.)	*Exploring Mathematical Ideas*—Ginn
5. big—little		*Enrichment Program I-II-III* (Ginn & Co.)
6. whole—part		*Growing Up With Numbers I-III* (McCormick, Mathers)
7. less than—more than		*How Big is a Foot*—Myller (Atheneum)
B. Fractions (concept of one-half)	Use simple fractions (for cooking, recipes, measurement	*The First Book of Measurement*— Epstein (Watts)
C. Measurements:	Use bottles, containers, measuring cups, scales, etc.	Relationship Cards (Ideal School Supplies Chicago, Ill.)
1. inch and foot	Explore terms of weight, size, amount	
2. calendar and clock	Use of ruler, yardstick	
3. money (cent, nickel, dime)	List amount of time spent daily at school, rest, play	
4. temperature	Read clock for classtime	

TABLE 12 (*Continued*)
ARITHMETIC

Units	Activities	Materials
	Read date from calendar Make a calendar; recognize day, week, month, year	*Filmstrips* *Time and Money* (McGraw Hill) *Fractions* (Colonial) *Making Change* (McGraw Hill)
D. Geometric (recognition of basic geometric forms	Show geometric forms (house, barn, orange, clock, boxes, cones, etc.)	*Hour and Half Hour* (McGraw Hill) *The Story of Money* (McGraw Hill) *Working with Fractions* (Colonial) *Measuring Time and Space* (Colonial) *Playing With Numbers* (Colonial) *Minutes* (McGraw Hill) *How Many in All* (Eye Gate) *How Many Are Left* (Eye Gate)
		Films *Let's Measure* (*Ounces, Pounds, Tons*) (Coronet Films) *Let's Measure* (*Pints, Quarts, Gallons*) (Coronet Films) *Old Woman in a Shoe* (Coronet) *Subtraction for Beginners* (EBF) *Ten Little Indians* (EBF) *Calendar—Weeks, Months, Days* (Coronet Films)

AREA V—SCIENCE

Answers to the how, what, and why of the physical world are part of all learning experiences. Children learn about pets; they observe simple changes in the weather; they discover that plants and animals live almost everywhere because they are in direct contact with them; they discover that the earth is made up of air, water, and land. Additionally, visiting markets, stores, trucking firms, dairies, and farms provide clues to understanding that our food comes from plants and animals and that there is need for helpers of many kinds. Ultimately we would hope that these students will be able to answer more questions about the world in which they live through a simple and realistic approach to scientific phenomena.

TABLE 13
SCIENCE

Units	Activities	Materials
I. Things That Live In Our World A. Animals	Children bring pets to school Incubation of chicks Classroom pets (white mice, hamsters, chameleons, birds, turtles, fish) Visits to zoos, farms, museums (prehistoric animals) Discuss use of animals for pleaslre, food, work Make scrapbook of animals Draw pictures of animals Discuss proper care of pets Build model zoo of farm in classroom	*The New I Wonder Why* (Holt, Rhinehart & Winston) *Science for Children K-3* (State U. of New York) *Science is Exploring* (Scott Foresman) *Science Far and Near* (D. C. Heath) *Exploring Science* (Allyn Bacon) *When You Go to the Zoo*—Blough (McGraw Hill) *Prehistoric Zoo*—Fenton (Doubleday) *The True Book of Animal Homes*—Podendorf (Childrens Press) *Animals in Winter*—Bancroft (Crowell) *Zoo Celebrities*—Bridges (Wm. Morrow Co.) *True Book of Animal Babies*—Podendorf (Childrens Press) *Big Book of Pets*—Green (Watts)
B. Insects	Draw spiders and webs Discuss the ant, bee colony life Discuss harmless vs. dangerous insects (tarantula, black widow spider) Discuss pest control, danger of insecticides How insects help us	*Insect Friends*—Teale (Dodd, Mead) *Insects and Plants*—Adler (John Day) *Insects and Their World*—Fenton (John Day) *All About the Insect World*—Love (Random House) *The Busy Little Honey Bee* (Rand McNally)

TABLE 13 *(Continued)*
SCIENCE

Units	Activities	Materials
		How and Why Wonder Book of Ants and Bees (Wonder Books)
		Golden Stamp Book of Insects (Golden Books)
		Farm Helpers—Payton (Melmont Pub.)
		Real Book About Farms—Howard (Watts)
		Let's Go to a Farm—Sootin (Putnam)
		Perhaps I'll Be a Farmer—Bethers (Aladdin Books)
		Wonderful World of Food—Boyd-Orr (Garden City Book)
C. Sea life	Make shell collections	*All About the Sea*—(Random House)
	Discuss edible seafoods	*Seashells* (Wonder Books)
	Trip to seashore	*Sea and Shore*—Hylander (MacMillan)
	Drawings of fish	*Sea and Sam*—Reed (Harcourt & Brace)
	Classroom aquarium	*Sea Shells*—Dudley (Cromwell)
	Mammals of the sea	*Seals and Walruses*—Darling (Morrow)
	Discuss how fish swim, breathe	*Here Come the Seals*—Goudey (Scribners)
	Breed guppies	*Life in Shallow Waters* (Doubleday)
		The First Book of Fish—Bendick (Watts)
		All About Fish—Burger (Random House)

TABLE 13 (*Continued*)
SCIENCE

Units	Activities	Materials
D. Birds	Discuss birds as pets (wild birds) Discuss bird migration Build bird houses, bird feeders Discuss how birds fly Discuss nest building Discuss mother's care of baby birds Show pictures of local birds, birds from other places	*Bird Watchers and Bird Feeders*—Blough (Whittlesey House) *Birds and Their World*—Fenton (John Day) *Birds We Live With*—Fenton (John Day) *First Book of Birds*—Williamson (Watts) *Birds In Their Homes*—Webb (Garden City Pub.) *Birds Eat and Eat and Eat*—Gans (Crowell) *True Book of Birds We Know*—Friskey (Childrens Press)
E. Reptiles and amphibians	Snakes as pets (poisonous snakes) How snakes are helpful to man The growth of the tadpole Ducks and geese Visit duck farm	*The Strange World of Reptiles*—Schmidt (Putnam) *Age of Reptiles*—Shuttlesworth (Garden City Books) *Reptiles and Amphibians*—Zim (Simon & Schuster) *Reptiles and Their World*—Felton (John Day) *The Book of Reptiles and Amphibians*—Bevans (Doubleday)

TABLE 13 (*Continued*)
SCIENCE

Units	Activities	Materials
F. Plants	Build classroom terrarium Plant bulbs, seeds Grow flower or vegetable garden Grow carrot tops, beet tops, sweet potatoes, etc. Discuss how plants help man Discuss what plants need to live Discuss the evergreen Identify types of trees	*Seeds Are Beautiful*—Foster (Melmont) *How Plants Grow*—Gray (American Book Co.) *Green is for Growing*—Lubell (Rand McNally) *True Book of Plants We Know*—Miner (Childrens Press) *Plants That Feed Us*—Fenton (John Day) *Plants, Food, and People*—Fenton (John Day) *Trees* (Row Petersen) *Leaves* (Row Peterson) *Science Problems* (Scott Foresman) *Science Today and Tomorrow* (Ginn & Co.) *What Science Is* (N.Y. State Dep't. of Ed.) *Hammond's Illustrated Nature Giude* (C. S. Hammond Co.)
II. Weather, Climate, Seasons, Temperature	Keep weather charts Discuss effect of weather on clothing choice Discuss effect of weather on daily activities Discuss clouds, fog, types of precipitation	*The Sun, The Wind, The Sea and The Rain*—Schlein (Abelard-Schuman) *All Ready For Winter*—Elgin (Jr. Literary Guild & McKay) *When Winter Comes*—Fox (Reilly & Lee)

TABLE 13 (*Continued*)
SCIENCE

Units	Activities	Materials
	Weather forecasting	*Winter Science Activities*—Youngpeter (Holiday House)
	Make simple wind vanes	*Winter Sleepers*—Sarasy (Prentice-Hall)
	Keep temperature charts	*Fall Is Here* (Row Peterson)
	Make and fly kites	*Winter-Sleeping Wildlife*—Barker (Harper Row)
	Discuss wind, movement of air	*Weather In Your Life*—Adler (John Day)
	Study weather maps	
	Study world map and globe	*Our Changing Weather*—Fenton (Doubleday)
	Listen to weather on radio, television broadcasts	*First Book of Weather*—Wyler (Watts)
	Read weather reports in newspapers	*All About Weather*—Tonehill (Random House)
	Discuss climate areas of the world	*Exploring the Weather*—Garland (Garden City)
	How the seasons provide recreation	*About Our Weather*—Gibson (Melmont)
	Holidays that go with seasons	
	How weather effects choice of food, clothing, fun around the world; the Eskimo, the Arab	*Real Book About Weather*—Forrester (Garden City)
	Discuss signs of changing seasons	*Everyday Weather and How it Works*—Schneider (McGraw Hill)
	Class mural of the four seasons	
	Discuss shape and rotation of earth, lead into seasons, length of year	*The True Book of Weather Experiments*—Podendorf (Childrens Press)
	Draw moon phases	*Hot and Cold*—Adler (John Day)
		Planet Earth—Wyler (Schuman Pub. Co.)

TABLE 13 (*Continued*)
SCIENCE

Units	Activities	Materials
III. The Universe A. Earth		*Planet Trip*—Nephew (Putnam) *The Nine Planets*—Branley (Cromwell) *All About the Planets*—Lauber (Random House) *What is the Earth*—Darby (Benefic Press) *What Is the Solar System*—Darby (Benefic Press) *A Book of Planets For You*—Branley (Crowell) *How and Why Wonder Book of Stars* (Wonder Books) *Let's Go to a Planetarium*—Wolfe (Putnam) *The Sun and Its Family* (Row Petersen) *The Sun* (Wm. Morrow) *A Child's Book of Stars* (Maxton Pub. Co.) *Fun With Astronomy* (Random House) *We Read About the Earth and Space*—Tannenbaum and Stillman (Gardner Pub.)

TABLE 13 (*Continued*)
SCIENCE

Units	Activities	Materials
B. Solar system	Draw solar system Visit planetarium if possible Bring in telescope Draw nine planets, color Make models of solar system Discuss and locate major constellations	*Space*—Holsaert (Holt, Rhinehart, & Winston) *The First Book of Space Travel*—Bendick (Watts) *Satellites in Outer Space*—Asimov (Random House) *Space Book for Young People*—Newell (McGraw Hill) *Book of Moon Rockets for You*—Branley (Crowell) *Project Mercury*—Coombs (Morrow)
C. Space travel	Write science fiction stories Draw and construct rockets Discuss possibilities of future space travel Discuss astronauts, United States space program Watch launching of space vehicles on television	*True Book of Space*—Podendorf (Childrens Press) *Go—The Story of Outer Space*—Verral (Prentice-Hall) *Space Wonders*—Golden Stamp Book (Simon & Schuster) *The Book of Moon Rockets for You*—Branley (Crowell) *The Moon Seems to Change*—Branley (Crowell) *What the Moon is Like*—Branley (Crowell) *A Look at the Moon*—Podendorf (Childrens Press) *The Moon: Our Neighboring World*—Binder (Golden Press)

Chapter 4

The Junior High School Special Class for Retarded

ADELE PAYERLE

INTRODUCTION

The ages thirteen through sixteen represent a very special time in the life of a teen-ager. It follows, therefore, that school during that period of time would be exciting, interesting, and very important. I have found this to be true of the retarded adolescent as well as the normal adolescent. Obviously, there is a great need for a good junior high special class situation. This time span serves as the bridge to close the gap between childhood and elementary school and the young adult ready to go out to secure and hold a job. Experience has shown that this is often a time of great conflict, sometimes greater than that for the normal adolescent. Chronological age and physical size makes people demand things of my children that they are either not ready to do or may never be capable of doing.

Many of my higher level children have sensed this, and thus there is conflict and anxiety which they must be helped to overcome. I try in my class to be as open and straightforward about this problem as I can. We often discuss their limitations and explore methods of handling them. As do all children, my youngsters react most favorably when I do not try to pull the wool over their eyes but rather accept them for what they are.

Utilizing this philosophy of teaching special class has presented me with a pedagogical problem, however, that I must always be aware of. How does one structure a classroom situation so that there is freedom for the children to be what they are and yet keep it realistic enough to make their behavior transferable to the

131

"outside world." For example, I have noticed that the most out-going and aggressive child in my class is lost in the crowd when he is with his friends in the regular student body. Observations such as these make me realize how unrealistic it is to keep these children in a special classroom. Upon this theory I base my jus-tification of placing them in regular nonacademic classes where they will have to adjust their behavior to the regular mainstream such as they will have to do on the job all of their lives.

Statistics have shown that retarded adults get lost in the main-stream of life in a community as adults and if we are going to educate them in school we have an obligation to make it as real-istic as possible.

I try to carry this philosophy over into my curriculum. I have taken each subject area and tried to pull from it the most useful information that will enable these children to function in the normal world.

ARITHMETIC

Arithmetic is an area that my children enjoy and in which they often experience success. As I mentioned before, I try to make this as functional as possible and this I think accounts for the high degree of enthusiasm and success (especially the work done with money). One thing that has helped so much is the fact that by the time these youngsters reach the junior high level they are handling money individually so much more. Their mothers are now sending them to the store alone and they must count change. Some of my children travel by bus and train and pay their own fares. I try to keep as many as these situations as I can in the front of my mind and assimilate them into the classroom situa-tion.

A great motivating factor in studying math of course is the idea of having their own jobs in the tenth grade. Preparing them with the skills to figure out their salary checks etc. has proven to be quite an adventure for these young people.

My approach to teaching math to the special class is to equip the children with as many skills as possible to enable them to handle any situation that they may come in contact with either on the job, at home, in a store, with personal allowances, or pub-lic vehicles.

TABLE 14
ARITHMETIC

Units	Activities	Materials

I. Time
A. Ability to understand various concepts of telling time:
  1. relationship of small hand and large
  2. fact of 60 min. = 1 hour
  3. fact of 30 min. = ½ hour
  4. fact of 15 min. = ¼ hour
B. Ability to tell time by quarter hour
C. Ability to tell time past half hour
D. Ability to express time in more than one way
E. Ability to understand minutes
F. Ability to express time in writing
G. Ability to add up hours
H. Concept of group of hours
I. Ability to subtract time
J. Concept of punctuality
K. Ability to set and wind clock
L. Relationship of time and money earned
	A. Learning to set an alarm clock
	Making individual clocks
	Lessons in workbook
	Ditto sheet lessons
	Practice writing school passes
	Game—"Around the Baseball Clock"
	Work with groups of individuals
	Using flash cards
	Have students work clock manually
	Practice setting own watches
	Keep notes in notebook
	Practice "punching" time clock
	Make up work charts comparing time and labor
	Play act imaginary work situations:
	  1. reporting late
	  2. not reporting
	  2. lunch hour
	  4. overtime
		alarm clock
		watch
		teacher-prepared dittoes
		flash cards
		teacher-prepared time cards
		Lennes' Essentials of Arithmetic (workbook)
		The Modern Practice Book in Arithmetic (Steck Co.)

II. Money
A. Concept of individual coins
  1. concept of dollar
  2. concept of change
	A. Buy school lunches
	Regular workbook lessons
	Practice buying things in school store
	Game—"Hangman"
		flash cards with money problems
		actual coins: pennies; nickels; dimes; quarters; half dollars; one, five, and ten dollar bills

TABLE 14 (Continued)
ARITHMETIC

Units	Activities	Materials
3. relationship of coins to each other 4. concept of dollar composed of parts	Work with individuals and groups using actual coins Buy and sell imaginary things	Lennes' Essentials of Arithmetic (Regular workbook) menus
B. How to make change by addition and subtraction C. Understanding of money value above one dollar D. Understanding of how to make change above one dollar E. Ability to read, understand, and solve money problems (buying and selling) F. Concept of money and labor G. Ability to write amounts of money in words	Make pot holders and sell them to faculty and students Maintain class treasury Work with money and work charts Make individual budgets Read menus and figure up bills—also grocery	newspaper ads teacher-prepared ditto sheets charts on working time and money earned time cards (teacher-prepared) food bills The Modern Practice Book in Arithmetic (Steck Co.)
III. Arithmetic Skills A. Addition 1. ability to add a three-digit number without carrying 2. ability to add a three-digit number with carrying 2. ability to add a four-digit number without carrying 4. ability to add a four-digit number with carrying 5. ability to add five-digit numbers	A. Workbooks Ditto sheet lessons Buying and making change in various phases of school life Keep written budgets in our notebooks Practice writing large numbers in words	coins Making Sure of Arithmetic (Silver Burdett Co.) The Modern Practice Book in Arithmetic (Steck Co.) flash cards Lennes' Essentials of Arithmetic (regular workbook) teacher-prepared ditto sheets

TABLE 14 (Continued)
ARITHMETIC

Units	Activities	Materials

B. Money symbols
  1. ability to add columns of dollars and cents
  2. correct placement of dollar sign and decimal point
  3. change from ¢ sign to decimal point
C. Placement of commas in correct places
D. Reading and writing large numbers
E. Subtraction
  1. ability to subtract with borrowing
  2. ability to subtract with money signs
  3. ability to subtract with 2, 3, 4 digits with borrowing
F. Multiplication
  1. understanding of multiplication tables 2-9
  2. concept of multiplication
  3. ability to multiply two digits: $\begin{array}{r}2\\ \times 2\\ \hline\end{array}$
	Figure out food menu and grocery bills	orange sticks
		playing cards

Note: Most of the skills that are learned are covered in our two workbooks; however, these skills are integrated into every feasible area in every subject.

TABLE 14 (*Continued*)

Units	Activities	Materials
4. ability to multiply four digits without carrying: $\begin{array}{r} 22 \\ \times 44 \\ \hline \end{array}$		
5. ability to multiply four digits with carrying		
6. ability to multiply five digits with carrying		
7. ability to multiply six digits with carrying		
8. ability to incorporate money symbols into multiplication		
9. ability to read and solve problems using multiplication		
G. Counting by 2, 3, 4, 5, etc.		
H. Understanding short division concept		
I. Concept of measuring 1 ft; $\frac{1}{2}$ ft; 1 yd.; 2 ft; 1 in.; $\frac{1}{4}$ in.		
J. Concept of mailing stamps, postage, etc.		
K. Use of ruler and yardstick		
L. Simple fractions and their use		

LANGUAGE ARTS

Since talking is the method of communication used most easily by retardates, the emphasis placed on this can never be too great. We discuss everything that the youngsters want to in my class. Many times I have had something else planned and they want to discuss another topic of interest and importance to them. In such instances we just talk! I search for such areas as correct use of grammar, sentence structure, ability to listen, sticking to the topic, and ability to contribute.

As far as written communication is concerned, this goes on continuously in all classes. I have listed in my curriculum the specific goals that I hope to reach in this area. Again, the correct use of grammar, sentence structure, and sticking to the topic are what we primarily seek.

TABLE 15
LANGUAGE ARTS

Unit	Activity	Materials
I. *Oral Communication*	A. Discussions of current events	newspapers
A. Ability to express himself in sentences acceptable to adults	Notes on current events	magazine articles
B. Freely discusses experiences (individually or with a group)	Directed discussions on tops of interest and importance are held as often as seems necessary	want ads
C. Ability to discuss current events	Structured telephone conversations	filmstrips
D. Ability to control or eliminate slang expressions	Play act job interviews	textbooks
E. Ability to describe directions	Message communication (students are freely sent throughout the building)	maps (student-made)
F. Carry on discussion pertinent to present conversation without changing the topic	Structuring situations where school and personal manners can be practiced	
G. Uses parts of speech correctly		
H. Notices speech mistakes in others		
II. *Written Communication*	A. Send postcards to friends and relatives	notebooks (loose leaf)
A. Writing correspondence	Practice writing thank-you notes	writing or note paper envelopes
1. write short notes	Weekly exercises with spelling words—sentences	*I Want to Learn English* (Steck Co.) (regular workbook)
2. write postcards	Regular workbook lessons	*New Goals in Reading* (Steck Co.)
3. address envelopes	Ditto sheet lessons	teacher-prepared ditto sheets and lessons
4. create simple sentences	Practice writing paragraphs	core vocabulary list
5. express thoughts in complete sentences	Look up words in dictionary	vocational vocabulary list
B. Grammar	Practice using a telephone book	telephone book
1. correct use of capitals:	Write letters to friends and pen pals	postcards
a. names		application blanks
b. months		

TABLE 15 (Continued)
LANGUAGE ARTS

Unit	Activity	Materials
c. days	Practice writing letters of application	
d. holidays	Weekly reading units, answering questions	
f. letters, etc.	Read in reading books, (groups and individuals)	
2. correct use of comma	Alphabetize spelling words (weekly)	
3. correct use of period		
4. correct use of question mark		
5. ability to use a quotation mark		
6. ability to use abbreviations		
C. Use of pen		
D. Script writing		
E. Spelling		
1. use of initials		
2. accurate spelling of vocabulary words		
3. 5-10 new spelling words per week		
4. use of dictionary		
5. use of telephone book		
F. Composition		
1. compose a paragraph		
2. compose a friendly letter		
3. compose a letter of application		
G. Understanding of synonyms		
H. Use of alphabetical order		
I. Correct use of capital letters		
J. Good telephone manners		
K. Breaking words into syllables		

OCCUPATIONAL INFORMATION

This special five month unit is perhaps the most important area of study in the junior high school class for the retarded. Many of these children have no concept of what it is like to work for money. I have found that like most children they think in terms of their parents taking care of them all of their lives.

This is the first idea that we have to dispel in teaching this unit. Once this has been accomplished we begin to introduce various skills and techniques that they will enhance upon and use in the high school while actually on the job.

Much of this work is taught through discussion as well as written assignments. The biggest problem is in motivating these children to want to find out about the world of work.

I find this subject interesting to teach because it is so necessary for the futures of my children. Breaking the total group into grades has helped a great deal—the ninth graders being more interested than the seventh. This I feel is because the goal is within sight, i.e. they will soon be graduating to the high school work study program.

TABLE 16
OCCUPATIONAL INFORMATION

Unit	Activity	Materials

I. Aspects of Employment
A. Ways of obtaining a job
B. Ways of holding a job
C. Qualities necessary for employment
D. Preparing for the job
E. Studying the type of job in terms of individuals' ability
F. Applying for job
  1. knowledge of job application forms
  2. knowledge of Massapequa area in terms of street names, traveling, etc.
G. Budgeting—ways of handling money
H. Getting along with family and friends
I. Getting along in the neighborhood
J. Areas of recreation in Massapequa
K. Personal hygiene
L. Relationships with other people
M. Traveling to and from the job
	A. Read want ads
	Answer job ads
	See filmstrip concerning different jobs
	Using workbooks and doing written exercises
	Fill out working papers
	Fill out job application forms
	Make up budgets
	Make job interest forms
	Make maps of local area
	Ditto sheet work
	Play act problems concerning work
	Locate signs for jobs around town
	School nurse lectures about personal hygiene
		The Jobs you Get (Workbook)
		teacher-prepared ditto sheet
		Rochester Occupation and Reading Series (Individual Jobs)
		application blanks
		working papers
		filmstrips
		maps
		newspapers (want ads)
		"Your Body and How It Works" and "Let's See" (Student Booklet)—Owen Publishing Charts

SOCIAL STUDIES

I teach social studies as a five month unit. The unit is broken down into three main areas: Massapequa government, county government, and Long Island government. Under each of these main headings I pull that information which is most functional and important for the present as well as the future. I try to tie as much information as possible in with occupations and the possibility of jobs but this I find is limited to Massapequa. Under Nassau County and Long Island, I try to cover the government— how it is run and how it affects our daily lives.

In teaching social studies it is important to cover local and county governments. Occupational information complements the social studies unit.

TABLE 17
SOCIAL STUDIES

Unit	Activity	Materials
I. Your District	Read in textbook	filmstrips
A. Places of importance in your district	Write notes in notebook	Encyclopedia-Britannica
	Show filmstrips	charts
B. Methods of town travel	Make individual maps	maps—teacher and student-prepared
C. Manners while traveling	Answer chapter questions	pictures
D. Paying fares on public vehicles	Read newspaper	ditto sheets
E. Learn about local shopping centers	Make charts showing various methods of transportation and communication	
F. Places of recreation	Send to county seat for materials	
G. Early history	Make comparison charts showing roles of governments	
H. Transportation facilities	Also field trips to bank, town hall, city hall, etc.	
I. Street names in town		
J. Ability to give verbal directions using names		
K. Ability to find limited number of areas on local map		
L. Role of teen-ager in his area		
M. Employment possibilities in local area		
II. County Government		
A. Early formation of county		
B. Early history of county		
C. Government of county		
D. Government in relation to our county		
E. Role of residents in local government		

INTEGRATION AND THE JUNIOR HIGH SCHOOL
SPECIAL CLASS

Working under the assumption that social development is as important as academic growth, if not more so at times, we have all of the special class youngsters placed in regular nonacademic subjects throughout the course of a normal school day. These courses include physical education, music, art, industrial arts, and home economics. As stated before these courses are of a nonacademic nature stressing the physical skills as opposed to strict intellectual achievement. Experience has shown that the retarded youngsters have been able to function on a satisfactory enough basis to warrant their placement in these classes. The teachers involved are notified of the presence of special class children and are usually most cooperative. The basic understanding that allows any measure of success is that these youngsters cannot possibly compete on the same level as normal children. However, just being in the same room, sitting next to and working with other youngsters at their own rate of speed has proven to be a more realistic situation in terms of life in general than the highly structured, confining special class room.

A. *Physical Education.* Development of character and mental and emotional qualities go hand in hand with good physical development. The retarded youngsters are exposed to everything in the program and participate to the extent of their individual abilities. Some of the activities offered are volleyball, field hockey, tumbling, gymnastics, and soccer. The experience of being dependent upon and in turn depended upon by classmates has been a good preparation for the work situation that they encounter in the high school. Many times children with lower IQ's are porrly coordinated and require extra physical training. With the cooperation of the members of the physical education department, we have been better able to provide a well-rounded educational experience for these children.

B. *Home Economics.* This is a course designed to equip girls and boys with those skills necessary to function better in the home. These children can now correctly set a table, make a good cup of coffee, cook a simple meal, read simple cooking instructions, and handle simple cooking measurements as well as many other skills. In this course they are also exposed to units on good grooming, baby care, and babysitting. At least once during the semester a luncheon is given for faculty members by the home economics classes. This has provided the experience of preparing for such an event and acting as a host or hostess.

C. *Industrial Arts.* Industrial arts is an important part of the curriculum for the special class boys. There are several different types of shops but we have met with the most success in the area of woodworking. Here the boys are taught to use many tools and machines that they will come in contact with either on the job or at home. These include the following:

1. screwdrivers
2. bits
3. braces
4. nails
5. chisels
6. clamps
7. brushes, varnishes
8. dowels
9. drills
10. planes
11. squares
12. rules and yardsticks

There have been few problems concerning the safety of these boys using the electric tools. However, the use of these tools is left entirely to the discretion of the teacher. I give him as much information as possible about a student but he makes the final decision as to what he can and cannot do.

D. *Art and Music.* Special class students are enrolled in art and music classes primarily for the social contacts that are made and the development of simple cultural experiences. Retarded youngsters seem to enjoy music and respond well to it. There have been some problems in the area of reading and writing. The primary activities in general music are listening, singing, and learning about music of the past. These areas have met with a high degree of success. In art class we have tried to gear the activities toward crafts. There is a high degree of skill and the caliber of the finished articles has shown a remarkable degree of skill. For those students who are capable of participating, a field trip to a museum is a highlight of the year.

Chapter 5

The Preparation and Placement of the Educable Retardate (Work - Study Program)

Arthur M. Hecht

THE preparation of young children is complete only if it concerns itself with the child's eventual entrance into the world of work with his successful adjustment to jobs, home life, and a compatible, satisfying social group life. A work-study program discharge its role most adequately when it concerns itself with the social and occupational adjustments in adult life.

Experience is an essential to successful adjustment to the work world. This calls for skills in filling out an application blank, getting along with employers, and mixing well with fellow employees. It is incumbent upon the school to guide these children and give them the wherewithal to satisfy these fundamental needs. To serve the retarded, we need information—much more information than now exists concerning the unskilled jobs which best fit them. This information is only useful and meaningful if it can be garnered and then passed along to the teachers, "the umbilical cord to the fetus."

To best help the retarded, we must develop sensible and practical yet remunerative goals which will aid the child in his quest for independence. Not many good work-study programs exist today. This chapter offers one from a practical working mold which pragmatically has proved itself; it works.

Some questions always face the schools: Can they help the parents accept the child as he is and not as they would like him to be? Can they mold him where possible to make the transition

147

from functioning student to good worker and to healthy, productive citizen?

We can leave nothing to chance in planning an educational program for the mentally retarded. If the world at large makes heavy demands upon the child socially, physically, vocationally, psychologically, and at times academically, we must keep abreast of those demands and serve as a procrustean bed, sensitive to the changing needs of the child in an everchanging world.

In setting up a program, the educational goals must focus upon some basic questions:

1. Does the supervised work benefit the student, the school, and the community? (It should benefit all.)

2. What is the best age group to considere? (16-18)

3. How long should a student spend in a specific training area? (As determined by teachers and employers, the average time seems to be one year on the job, out of an average three year work-study program.)

4. How should the student split his time? (3 hours in school; 3 hours on the training job.)

5. How much obligation does the employer have? (It depends. Some employers want no obligations to take the student on for later employment; others are quite willing to commit themselves to the fruition of the program.)

6. Can the employer "pull out?" (Any time he so desires.)

7. Is the employer reimbursed? (Yes, through the Division of Vocational Rehabilitation if the services of DVR are utilized.)

8. What will the cost be to the school district? (All testing of the child is done by the school personnel at no cost to the school district.)

9. Who handles any forms and reports that may be required? (The work-study teacher.)

10. Who is the best liaison with the employer concerning any problems that may arise? (The work-study teacher of the special class.)

11. What essentially are the best objectives of a secondary program for the adolescent educable mentally retarded? (Economic self-sufficiency and civic responsibility.)

12. What type of employees are the employer seeking? (Neat, punctual students who complete tasks, work well with others, and assume responsibilities in accordance with their abilities.)

A STEP BY STEP APPROACH TO SETTING UP A WORK-STUDY PROGRAM

Special education at the junior and senior high school levels is aimed towards students within the 50-75 I.Q. range, as required by almost every law.

In the junior high prework study classes, the emphasis is placed upon a citizenship education core program with stress on academic materials to meet individual mental abilities of the students, especially in travel, communication, and preparation for employment.

After having attained the age of sixteen and having been evaluated by the special education team of teachers, administrators, and psychologists, and having been found to meet some basic criteria, the student is ready for the world of work. These criteria include the following:

1. academic achievement level
2. emotional stability
3. social maturity
4. physical examination

The curriculum for these senior class students is actually an extension of the junior high school program with emphasis on oral expression in language instruction to be able to give and ask for simple directions and common, everyday classroom activities in written expressions such as a job application, maintaining household budgets, and simple banking forms. Spelling needs would be directed to the student's job opportunities as well as towards meeting minimum standards for understanding industrial forms such as time cards, employment payroll blanks, and simple medical forms. Basically, therefore, the curriculum is a core program integrating subject matter which is dependent upon interests, needs, abilities, chronological age, and the physical, social, and intellectual development of the child.

Students in the work-study group will extend their mathematics knowledge by stressing the use of money and making change. Basic budget items related to household expenses such as rent, groceries, taxes, clothing, and savings will be explored and evaluated. The social studies area of the curriculum should encompass the city and community at large, discuss and study job areas, explore ways of getting and holding a job and spending one's income wisely. Another area of the curriculum which educators have successfully experienced with over the years, is health education. Through such education the students gain a more comprehensive knowledge of the human body as well as familiarity with simple medical terms.

The regular shop, physical education, and home economics programming should remain constant. A good special education teacher will incorporate them into the program by urging regular teachers to accept the children. Such integration of subject areas makes a world of difference in maintaining a successful program.

All students should be assigned to regular homerooms according to age and normal grade expectancy. The higher level functioning educable retardate should be given the opportunity to participate in regular classes such as personal typing, advanced shops, driver education, and introduction to business. This gives the students a sense of belonging and getting to know their fellow students with whom they will live side by side in the world.

After curriculum and administrative guidelines have been drawn up, the role of the parents must be clearly ascertained. A general meeting should be held each year with parents of employed students and parents of future work-study candidates. The entire program and its objectives should be explained and discussed in detail. Parental suggestions and reactions must be assessed and evaluated to have the optimal harmonious relationship between the home and the school.

Ultimate, however, it is the work-study teachers' responsibility to enlist the support of the local business community. A forthright and frank appraisal of the abilities and disabilities of the students involved should be undertaken from the very outset. Visits to local service clubs, such as the Lions, Rotarians, and Kiwanis can be valuable in selling the program to local civic leaders. Joining a local service club in your school district and offering your services at speaking engagements can be valuable to the program as well.

A school day of three hours of instruction in the morning, a lunch hour, and three hours of actual employment time for the work-study student seems to work out best for the program.

Once the above steps are completed, the work-study teacher must analyze his students for placement. An initial evaluation of the student's interests and abilities combined with talents and personality is essential. This is our first phase in selling the prospective employer, and it should be done carefully before our job-choosing campaign. Our next step is to study the job situation in light of opportunities, working conditions, and prospects for full-time employment upon graduation. The more leads compiled and emloyers contacted, the more chances there are for finding the right job. The work-study coordinator is a salesman and like any good salesman, he must build a list of prospective customers. The more planning we put into our job-hunting campaigns, the better chance we give the student to get the right job.

After setting up our job portfolio, we inject into the curriculum as needed the following skills: understanding and filling out application blanks; reading, always a problem, is reinforced for better understanding of posters, newspaper ads, and want ads in local papers; and the costs of transportation within and out of the community are also studied. Socio-drama interviews, in which one pupil is the employer and the other the employee with the class evaluating the interviews, can be an excellent teaching tool. It has proven to be very popular with far-reaching results.

A re-evaluation of all the records and private counseling sessions with each student to redetermine their goals and decide on the most suitable job placement should be a natural follow up at this point. The selected students are then sent out on their interviews. If we have planned well in advance with the employer, the student will be hired. At this point, the work-study teacher usually visits the employer and sets up guidelines for weekly visits on the job.

Through his visits to on-the-job training sites and maintainence of relationships with his students and employers, the work-study teacher can be flexible and develop additional curriculum materials correlating experiences and problems the students find on the jobs. We can possibly offer additional training in skills, and can improve the student's abilities to adjust to the job situation. Always, of course, we stand ready to offer more guidance counseling where it may be required.

The work-study program is the bridge between school and work. The work-study teacher is responsible for soliciting job opportunities, supervising on-the-job training, participating in case conferences with the special education team, and developing curriculum that correlates with the student's work.

Armed with new interests and confidence derived from successful participation in normal society, the retarded student can be thought of as a human being with all the normal complexities, emotions, and interests we all experience who is ready to take his place in our society as a contributing member. Realistically, we must admit that there are always a few (fortunately a *very* few) students who can never be placed in private industry. Usually, severe emotional or physical problems serve to preclude effective placement for such children. We hope, however to dramatically cut down the numbers of such unplaceable children as the work-study programs achieve greater national and local acceptance and as we improve our knowledge and handling of the severely emotionally disturbed.

Also, the work-study teachers and school districts often have the services of the local State Department of Vocational Rehabilitation and the Association for Help of Retarded Children Workshops. These two organizations can and will provide a training program for mentally retarded workers who require supervised, sheltered workshop experience and training to overcome those limitations which hamper direct placement into competitive situations.

JOB PREPARATION THROUGH OCCUPATIONAL INFORMATION

I. A unit, perhaps one entitled "How People Live and Work in Our Community," may be presented to establish a background for learning about opportunities in your area and to help the students adapt to their future role as workers and citizens of our country.

II. Job opportunities are listed daily in the newspapers, and there is a moderate amount of competition for desirable positions. Most occupations require some previous knowledge or training. The teacher could begin by reading the want ads in the newspaper as though in search of a part-time job. The students may ask questions and a discussion can follow.

III. *Instructional material*
   A. A copy of the daily newspaper and a copy of *The New York Times* for comparison
   B. Chalk, blackboard
   C. Pictures of various occupations

IV. When the children show interest and ask questions, it is wise to pursue a unit such as the following at this time:
   A. How do people live and work in our area?
   B. Where are the places of interest in our neighborhood?
   C. What are the best ways to travel in our neighborhood?
   D. What are the facilities of the neighborhood, i.e., shopping, etc.?
   E. What are the employment possibilities?
   F. What are the recreational facilities?
   G. What are the health services in the community?

V. The teacher's objectives must concern themselves with the following:
   A. Developing successful social relationships by organizing the children into groups and by encouraging individual research activities
   B. Developing good work habits, i.e., completion of assign-

ments, listening to classmates' reports, and speaking
clearly when reporting orally

C. Developing respect for other children's contributions
and encouraging free expression in the group

D. Acquainting the children with specific facts concerning
the role of the citizens of our county

E. Achieving greater competency in reading for information, computation (determining dates and length of reports), and writing

F. Initiating a discussion of what jobs are available, who
applies for these positions, how they pay, etc., by reading want ads in the newspaper and thus spurring the
children's natural curosity (This will lead to further
study on the subject.)

VI. The planning and working periods
The teacher will pre-plan the unit carefully because of the
nature of the children.
The students will decide what they want to find out and
the teacher will guide this discussion.

VII. The children may take trips to the following places:

A. City Hall to visit the elected officials who make and en-
force the laws observed by the citizens of our community

B. Various factories, automotive works, and stores in their
area to see how people work and spend their money

C. Local parks to see how and where citizens spend their
leisure time

D. The local hospital to find out how people care for the
sick and needy
(*Note*: We will endeavor to use several means of transportation so that the children may be acquainted with
the modes of travel in their county.)

VIII. Evaluation techniques
With the mentally retarded, the following evaluation techniques might prove useful in determining the success or
failure of the methods of instruction:

1. objective observations by the teacher
2. oral testing for information (facts learned) during and at the end of the unit
3. oral group reports
4. teacher-made true and false quizzes where the teacher reads the question and the pupil writes "t" or "f"
5. observing and recording individual participation in classroom activities

A SUGGESTED OCCUPATIONAL EDUCATION PROGRAM

 I. What Types of Jobs Exist (e.g. auto, construction, hospital service)

 II. Knowing Job Requirements (how difficult, special skills needed, union regulations and dues, etc.)

 III. Ways To Get A Job
   A. References (friends, relatives, teachers)
   B. Answering want ads (distance from your home, hours, salary, social climate, security)
   C. Parents
   D. Agencies (employment, federal, public, private, special)

 IV. Things To Consider In Getting A Job
   A. Appearance (voice, manner, dress, poise)
   B. Punctuality
   C. Salary
   D. Working conditions
   E. Hours

 V. Holding a Job
   A. Skills (handling tools, punctuality, good attendance, conscientiousness)
   B. Character traits (friendly, polite, self-control, honesty, ready to learn, ability to take criticism, desire to improve, etc.)

VI. Forms and Blanks
  A. Applications (telephone, letter, in person interview, social security)
  B. Work permits
  C. Banking (checking, savings, deposits, withdrawals, interest, writing checks to pay bills)
  D. Postal (change of address, money order, parcel post, etc.)

VII. Jobs Needing Special Training
  A. Barber and beautician
  B. Carpenters helper (plumber, electrician, mason, etc.)
  C. Civil service jobs (hospital, sanitation, postal, highway maintenance)

  I. What We Budget For (food, rent, clothing, recreation, health etc.)

  II. Ways of Buying (cash, installment, loan, etc.)

Third Year: Citizenship

  I. Getting Along With Others (manners, being honest, reliable, respecting rights of others, recognizing importance of parental advice, etc.)

  II. Taxes (income, residence, sales, property, school etc.)

  III. Voting Requirements (age residence, registration, etc.)

  IV. Civic Responsiblity (obey law, defend country, respect rights of others, etc.)

  V. Social Values (how to behave in a democracy, celebration of national holidays, etc.)

JOB PLACEMENT

Before placement on the job, the student's potential must be determined in an effort to see how well they mesh with the requirements of the job. Vocational aptitude tests, teachers' observations, students' interests and psychometric evaluations are all carefully weighed in determining the child's potential. The eventual choice of job is left to the student, although efforts are made to guide him toward the job which will best fit his needs.

A *teacher's evaluation of a prospective job* should carefully consider and include the following points:

1. the person interviewed
2. firm name and address
3. type of jobs
4. education needed
5. training
6. future prospects
7. salaries
8. desirable qualifications

A *student's evaluation of a prospective job (what the student would like to do)* should carefully and honestly answer the following questions:

1. What work interests you?
2. Why does it interest you?
3. What do you know about the job?
4. How would you get it?
5. What qualifications do you possess for this job?
6. How can you prove your qualifications (past employment, school work, outside activities)?

The student may want to do field work to familiarize himself with a job area. He may select several job areas; go to the library and papers to gain a knowledge of these jobs; list the jobs, and give his qualifications for them. In this way he may make the best choice for himself.

TABLE 18

RELATED MATERIALS AND SOURCES IN TEACHING THE MENTALLY
RETARDED ADOLESCENT

A Curriculum Source Reference for the
Development of a Work-Study Program

Source	Cost	Item
I. Vocational V.A. Pamphlet 5-16 V.A. Washington 5, D. C.	Free	Working on a Hospital Team
The Glidden Co. 900 Union Commercial Bld. Cleveland 14, Ohio	Free	Getting the Right Job
Socony Mobile Oil Co. 26 Broadway New York 4, N. Y.	Free	So You Want A Better Job
U.S. Dept. of Labor 341 9th Ave. New York, N. Y.	Free	From School to Work With Help
Changing Times 1729 H St., N.W. Washington 6, D.C.	Free	Job Interview—Handle It Right
Pasadena City Schools Pasadena, Calif.	Free	Work-Study Program Occupational Relations Course
Guidance Centre Ontario College of Education University of Toronto	$.20	Occupational information Monograph Service Station Attendant

TABLE 18 (*Continued*)
RELATED MATERIALS AND SOURCES IN TEACHING THE MENTALLY
RETARDED ADOLESCENT
A CURRICULUM SOURCE REFERENCE FOR THE
DEVELOPMENT OF A WORK-STUDY PROGRAM

Source	Cost	Item
Syracuse University Press Syracuse, New York	$1.00 ea.	Occupational Reading Series for Reluctant Readers
Noble & Noble Publishers New York, N. Y.	$1.55	Adult Education Series Book 2: Your Family and Your Job—Cass
Bellman Publishing Co. Box 172 Cambridge, Mass.	Free catalog	Occupational briefs
B'nai Brith Vocational Service 1129 Vermont Ave., N.W. Washington, D. C.	Free	Catalog on Vocational Literature
Chronicle Guidance Service Moravia, N. Y.	Free	Occupational Brief 2-27.01 2-27-99.25 Waiter, Waitress
Oakland Public Schools Oakland, Calif.	Free	How To Hunt A Job—Best Foot Forward
Westminster College New Wilmington, Pa.	Free	Land A Job And Hold It
New York State Employment Service (or local offices) Freeport, N. Y.	Free	Why Young People Fail to Get and Hold Jobs

TABLE 18 (*Continued*)

RELATED MATERIALS AND SOURCES IN TEACHING THE MENTALLY
RETARDED ADOLESCENT

A CURRICULUM SOURCE REFERENCE FOR THE
DEVELOPMENT OF A WORK-STUDY PROGRAM

Source	Cost	Item
Dept. of Public Relations General Motors Detroit 2, Michigan	Free	Can I Get the Job
American Cyanimid Co. Calco Chemical Division Bocide, Brooklyn, N. Y.	Free	How to Find the Right Job
Chronicle Guidance Publishers Moravia, N. Y.	$.25 ea.	Summer Jobs for Teenagers (Routeman and Taxi Driver)
American Trucking Association 1424 16 Street, N.W. Washington 6, D. C.	Free	Information
National Association of Motors Bus Operators 839 17th Street, N.W. Washington 6, D.C.	Free	Information
American Hotel Association 221 West 57th St. New York 19, N. Y.	Free	Information

TABLE 18 *(Continued)*

RELATED MATERIALS AND SOURCES IN TEACHING THE MENTALLY
RETARDED ADOLESCENT

A CURRICULUM SOURCE REFERENCE FOR THE
DEVELOPMENT OF A WORK-STUDY PROGRAM

Source	*Cost*	*Item*
National Restaurant Association 850 Michigan Ave. Chicago 3, Ill.	Free	Menus and information
Psychological Corp. New York, N. Y.	$2.20	Employee Evaluation Manual For Interviewers Fear and Jordan
U. S. Dept. of Labor	$1.00	Subscriptions for Occupations Outlook Reg. #964-1-22-58
New York State Employment Service Freeport, N. Y.	Free	Job Hunting How to Get and Hold the Right Job
Changing Times—Kiplinger Magazine 1729 H Street, N.W. Washington 6, D. C.	Free	How To Write Yourself Up
Science Research Associates, Inc. 57 W. Grand Ave. Chicago 10, Ill.	See catalog	Life Adjustment Booklets: Getting Job Experience How to Get the Job Our World of Work School Subjects and Jobs What Employers Want You and Unions

TABLE 18 (*Continued*)

RELATED MATERIALS AND SOURCES IN TEACHING THE MENTALLY
RETARDED ADOLESCENT

A CURRICULUM SOURCE REFERENCE FOR THE
DEVELOPMENT OF A WORK-STUDY PROGRAM

Source	Cost	Item
Ester O. Carsons Pasadena, Calif.	$1.65	Teen-Agers Prepare for Work Book I and Book II
II. Personal Appearance		
Science Research Associates 57 W. Grand Ave. Chicago 10, Illinois	See catalog	Guide to Good Grooming
Kimberley-Clark Corp. Neenah, Wisconsin	Free	Are You In The Know?
Educational Service Dept. Bristol-Myers Products Div. 45 Rockefeller Plaza New York 20, N. Y.	Free	Grooming at Your Service
III. Handling Money		
Time Inc. Rockefeller Center New York, N.Y.	$5.00	Study of Consumer Expenditures
Science Research Associates 57 W. Grand Ave. Chicago 10, Illinois	See catalog	Make Your Pennies Count Money and You

TABLE 18 *(Continued)*
RELATED MATERIALS AND SOURCES IN TEACHING THE MENTALLY
RETARDED ADOLESCENT
A CURRICULUM SOURCE REFERENCE FOR THE
DEVELOPMENT OF A WORK-STUDY PROGRAM

Source	Cost	Item
Household Finance Co. Chicago 11, Illinois	$.10	Booklets on money management
IV. Safe Living		
Employee Relations Inc. 13 E. 53 St. New York 22, N. Y.	Free	Home Safe Home
National Safety Council Dearborn Street Chicago, Ill.	Free	Request list of safety materials
Science Research Associates 57 W. Grand Ave. Chicago 10, Ill.	See catalog	Your Safety Manual
V. General Materials		
Local Chamber of Commerce	Free	Town, village, county maps
The Economic Press Inc. Montclair, New Jersey	Free	How You Can Write Better Letters

TABLE 18 (*Continued*)

RELATED MATERIALS AND SOURCES IN TEACHING THE MENTALLY
RETARDED ADOLESCENT

A Curriculum Source Reference for the
Development of a Work-Study Program

Source	Cost	Item
A.F.L. and C.I.O. 225 W. 34 St. New York, N. Y.	Free	Information on unions
Bell Telephone Co. Local Office	Free loan for two weeks	Teletrainer unit for teaching proper use of the telephone
Child Research Clinic Woods School Langhorne, Pa.	Free	The Adolescent Exceptional Child Faces Adulthood
National Society for Crippled Children and Adults 11 S. LaSalle St. New York, N. Y.	$1.00	Bulletin on current literature
National Association for Retarded Children 99 University Pl. New York, N. Y.	$1.15	Sheltered Workshops for Retarded Children
Equitable Life Insurance Co. Society of U.S. New York, N. Y.	Free	Ask for catalog of publications Materials on functional living

TABLE 18 *(Continued)*

RELATED MATERIALS AND SOURCES IN TEACHING THE MENTALLY
RETARDED ADOLESCENT

A CURRICULUM SOURCE REFERENCE FOR THE
DEVELOPMENT OF A WORK-STUDY PROGRAM

Source	Cost	Item
Milton Bradley Co. Springfield, Mass.	See catalog	Materials for teaching the exceptional children
Local gas stations	Free	State and local maps
U.S. Dept. of Health, Education and Welfare Office of Education Washington, D. C.	$.50	Curriculum Adjustments for the Mentally Retarded
VI. Travel and Vacationing American Automobile Association	Free	Guide to Vacationing
Greyhound Tours	Free	Travel data
New York State Chamber of Commerce Albany, N. Y.	Free	Vacationlands in New York

16 MM MOTION PICTURES ON SOCIAL LIVING AND ADJUSTMENT
Film Library
Yeshiva University
187 St. & Amsterdam Ave.
New York, N. Y.

Title	Rental	Title	Rental
Making a Decision in the Family	$2.50	Making a Decision	2.50
Leaving It to the Experts	3.00	Getting What You're After	3.00
Community Responsibility	3.00	Choosing a Leader	2.50
Manners in School	3.00	Being Different	3.00
Manners in Public	3.00	Toward Emotional Maturity	4.00
Joe's Roxy	7.00	Habit Patterns	4.00
Who is Sylvia	7.00	Facing Reality	4.00
American Girl	7.50	Understanding Cyphers	4.00
The Teens	7.00	The Troublemaker	4.00
Social Acceptability	6.00	The Snob	4.00
Discipline During Adolescence	5.00	The Procrastinator	3.00
Age of Turmoil	6.00	The Outsider	3.00
Baby-Sitter	4.50	The Griper	3.00
Who's Running Things	3.00	The Good Loser	4.00
One Man's Opinion	3.00	Cheating	3.00

FILMS ON OCCUPATIONAL INFORMATION

Food Service

Order #	Title	Cost	Source
TF10-1514	Service of Food	Free	United States Army
116	Restaurant Operator	Free	Vocational Guidance Films
TF10-1644	Mess Management	Free	United States Army
TF8-1500	Galley Sanitations	Free	United States Army
	Dishwashing Dividends	Free	School of Modern Photography
	Dishwashing by Hand	Free	Los Angeles Health Dept.
	Dishwasher Named Red	Free	General Food Products
TF8-1501	Disease and Personal Hygiene	Free	United States Army
118	America's Heritage of Hospitality	Free	National Restaurant Association
113	Introducing Alice	Free	Cornell College Dept. of Home Economics

Budgeting

Budgeting for Better Living	Free	Money Management Institute
Your Money's Worth in Shopping	Free	Household Finance Co.
Make Sense With Your Clothing	Free	See catalog
How to Stretch Your Food Dollar	Free	Prudential Plaza
How to Use Consumer Credit Wisely	Free	Prudential Plaza
Why Budget	Free	Prudential Plaza

Custodial

Title	Educational Film Guide
How to Wet Mop	LCF1 53-44
Janitor Training Series	LCF1 53-47
How to Brush, Sweep a Stairway	LCF1 53-45
How to Treat a Sweeping Mop	LCF1 53-46
How to Clean With a Dustmop	LCF1 53-48

OCCUPATIONAL STUDIES FILMS

Grooming

Title	Cost	Source
The Clean Look	Free	Assoc. Films
Heads Up for Beauty	Free	Assoc. Films
Improving Your Posture	$2.00	AMNH
Care of Skin	$2.50	EBF
Developing Friendships	$2.50	Ideal Films
Good Sportsmanship	$2.50	Ideal Films
Measure of a Man	Free	Assoc. Films
Friendly Way	Free	Assoc. Films
School Rules, How They Help Us	Free	Ideal Films
Habit Patterns	Free	Syracuse University
Prepare Through Education	Free	U. S. Army
Everyday Courtesy	Free	Ideal Films
You and Your Parents	Free	Ideal Films
Friendships Begin At Home	Free	Ideal Films
Choosing Your Occupation	Free	Ideal Films
Family Life	Free	AMNH
Benefits of Looking Ahead	Free	Ideal Films
Act Your Age	Free	Ideal Films
Are You Popular	Free	AMNH
A B C's of Hand Tools	Free	General Mtors Corp.

Addresses

Association Films (Assoc.)	Encyclopedia Brittanica Films
347 Madison Ave.	202 E. 44 St.
New York, N. Y.	New York 17, N. Y.
Ideal Films	
233 W. 42 St.	
New York, N. Y.	

Job Educational Films

How To Keep a Job	Ideal Films
Getting the Job	
Getting A Job	
The First Job	
Job Growth	McGraw Hill Co.
Adjusting to the Job	330 W. 42 St.
Your New Job	New York, N. Y.
Selling Yourself to An Employer	
Story of Packaging	
Art of Gift Wrapping	Assoc. Films

Filmstrips

The Job Interview	
Supermarket	
Waitress	
How To Use Your Checkbook	
Variety Store	
Nurses Aid	Eye Gate Company
Gas Station Attendant	New York, N. Y.

OCCUPATIONAL INFORMATION BOOKS

Occupational information: Baer and Roeber, Science Research Assoc., see catalog.

Handbook of Job Facts: Lechter, Science Research Assoc., 1962, see catalog.

Occupational literature: Forrester, H. W. Wilson Co., 1958, in guidance section of school library.

Occupational Brief: B'nai Brith Vocational Service, 1129 Vermont Ave., N.W., Washington, D. C., free.

   The following books cover work-study needs of special education and cover the curriculum in reading, English, math, etc. for the retarded:

Foundations of Citizenship I and

Foundations of Citizenship II: Bernard Shawn, Richards Press, Phoenix, N. Y.

Workbook I and II—Right, Duties, Citizenship: Cocoran, Richards Press.

Getting Ready for Payday, Richards Press.

Workbooks I, II, and III: Hudson and Weaver, Richards Press.

I Want a Job: Hudson and Weaver, Richards Press.

Job Analysis Series (gas station, supermarket, etc.): Syracuse Press, Syracuse Univ.

Chapter 6

A Sheltered Workshop Experience for the Mentally Retarded

MILTON LEVINE

PHILOSOPHY

THE Vocational Training Center and Workshop, a division of the Association for the Help of Retarded Children (AHRC), provides services and training on an "earn while you learn" basis in a number of industrial, commercial, and service fields to more than four-hundred clients annually. In a simulated factory, complete with machinery for blister-sealing, shrink-packing, heavy-duty stapling, drilling, and punching, mentally retarded adults learn light assembly and packaging operations on subcontracts from private industry while others receive training performing jobs in shipping, receiving, maintenance, and porter work. In addition, a complete commercial kitchen and cafeteria provide training in food services; our two greenhouses provide training areas for landscaping, and florist and greenhouse assistants; our administrative offices are utilized to offer practice in typing, mimeographing, addressing, switchboard, and receptionist activities; and our educational center offers an opportunity to train mentally retarded adults in child care within a school atmosphere.

Trainees learn to master a job in a relatively anxiety-free atmosphere which is conducive to trail-and-error problem solving as well as systematic, vocationally structured learning. It is a setting in which trainees can test their growth and learning with-

169

out the ordinary implications of failure overtaking them—ostracism from the group, total loss of wages, or ridicule. To the contrary, guidance and constructive criticism takes the place of consistent failure.

In addition to mastering a job, trainees learn to adapt to the physical stresses imposed by working a full day— perhaps in a standing position all day, perhaps repetitively making the same arm motion. They learn to adapt to the emotional stresses normally encountered in a work environment, by learning to cope with possible dislike of the "boss" and learning not to neglect their work to talk with a favorite friend. Additionally they must learn daily habits of attendance and punctuality, the repetitive and consistent performance of a work routine, and the ability to appropriately accept and carry out direction and supervision from others.

It is the philosophy of this Center that each specific job— whether at a machine or in another kind of work area—is merely a device to develop general concepts of work. We know the mentally retarded will most likely never be skilled workmen. We also know that if they are properly trained to follow daily routines consistenty and purposefully they can potentially enter the community labor force. We feel that the Center exemplifies the program of community action that President Johnson and President Kennedy urged through the President's Committee on Mental Retardation. All of our trainees, even those who continue to be sustained in a sheltered workshop, reach some level of remunerative employment. Through this wage-earning capacity, they gain in self-sufficiency and self-respect and add also to the total productivity and pride of the community to which they belong.

It should be noted that criteria for acceptance at the workshop is minimal in reference to level of retardation. There are no minimum I.Q. requirements; the individual need only be capable of sustaining his daily needs to be accepted for evaluation. *No* wage earning level is needed to be retained as an employee of the workshop nor are any individuals required to pay for a service they may receive from the agency.

INTAKE AND REFERRAL PROCEDURES

Intake

The initial intake is a significant and sensitive contact between a new client and the agency. The relationships established with the counselor help to determine the climate of adjustment. During this interview the nature of the agency is interpreted to the training and those who accompany him. At this time the needs, hopes, aspirations, likes, dislikes, and previous work exposures of the trainee are elicited to determine which training areas would be most effective for him. Additionally, the prospective trainee and his family are familiarized with the agency's rules and regulations and its expectations regarding the trainee's compliance with them.

A counselor administers this interview and assumes responsibility as liaison between this agency, the referral source and/or any other agency involved in servicing the client.

Referral

Inasmuch as the first meeting is a tone and pace-setter for the impressions the client and his family receive of the agency and for the impression the counselor receives of them, it is essential that all information regarding the prospective trainee be available to the center prior to intake. In this way, when the interview does take place, the counselor is aware of the client's history and can structure the interview appropriately.

General Information
1. Client's name, address, telephone number, age, and sex
2. Parents' or guardians' names and addresses, if different from above
3. Client's educational background
4. Summary of pertinent sociocultural data
5. Statement of services requested

Medical and Psychological Information
1. Summary of previous psychological workups and dates on which they took place are essential.
2. If psychiatric services have been used, summary of diag-

nostic and prognostic data plus information clearance slips
should also be available.

3. Summary of specific physical limitations and restrictions and
other limiting factors (e.g. sensory or motor impairments)
are also needed.

4. If client is currently followed by any other agency or clinic,
name of facility and nature of contact should be included.

5. If hospitalization of any kind has taken place, institution's
name, dates, and nature of admissions should be included.

6. All material from institutions, family doctor, or any other
pertinent sources are requested through parental written
authorization.

HISTORY OF WORKSHOPS

Workshops for the retarded were initiated by associations
created by parent groups seeking help for their retarded children.
The original concept was simply to provide a program to occupy
the time of those individuals for whom schooling was not available or for those over school age. Arts and crafts programs were
used as a method to fill the long days and to provide some creative aspect to the program.

As the associations grew in size and scope, a few professional
workers began to enter the field. These workers were primarily
in the psychosocial areas and had some background in the field
of rehabilitation. With the influx of the professional, the character of the crafts program began to change into a work-oriented
center engaged primarily in subcontracting small jobs from industry. The advent of this policy also changed the use of the work
center which could now provide industrial tasks and, in turn,
enable the center to provide realistic work for those who could be
trained for industry.

Today the workshop has two major functions: job training and
placement, and sheltered employment. Since the workshop could
accommodate real work, the clients could earn wages for work
produced, as required by the Federal Law, thereby creating
incentive and motivation to work.

Evaluation

The basic ingredients of the working world can now be presented to the retardate in their simplest forms. Naturally, some method of ascertaining the social and job skills of the retarded individual had to be instituted in order to determine his feasibility for job training or sheltered employment. The tools formerly utilized by the psychologist and social worker were combined with a new element of vocational evaluation. Psychological testing is interwoven with subjective observation and objective testing of the client's productivity in the form of quality and quantity of produced items.

If we look at any normal job, numerous life situations can be identified and brought into play as methods of observing social and work attitudes. These same situations found in a job are brought to bear on the retardate in the workshop. Unconscious or conscious behavior, as in relating to a foreman, supervisor, or boss, must be spelled out to the retarded client and, in turn, observed and evaluated by the staff during the course of his evaluation. What may normally appear to be obvious and necessary behavior on a job has to be interpreted to the client and occasionally tested by the workshop staff. It has become evident that proper work attitudes and adjustment to the work setting is the major concern of the workshop. Manual skills are of secondary importance, since experience has taught us that the primary cause of losing a job arises out of improper work attitudes and not lack of skill.

Quality and quantity control provide an objective method of obtaining skill levels needed to present sufficient data to a prospective employer and to evaluate productive speed, neatness, and work habits required in competitive industry. A lack of these skills indicates a warning to the investigators during the evaluation period; fluctuation in the number of items produced may signal some emotional design created by work pressures or movement from one operation to another. Physical disabiilties will become evident to the trained observer when the client must perform many different motions. In addition, emotional stress becomes evident when the client is placed into production line assembly operations requiring speed. Many other types of behavioral material can be observed by the mere contact of the client with supervisors or co-workers.

Pertinent data collected regarding the client's progress is assembled on check sheets and narrative type forms designed specifically for evaluation purposes. This material is utilized to formulate vocational plans to be instituted in the training phase of the workshop program.

Training

The workshop affords a unique opportunity to provide not only a realistic testing situation in regard to work potential but also provides the closest facsimile to an industrial setting yet available to the disabled. The environment of the workshop should be maintained in a strict industrial atmosphere allowing the disabled worker to initiate his own pace and gradually work up to maximum efficiency. By definition the Workshop is a nonprofit organization and therefore is able to provide a more relaxed atmosphere which can be used to increase or decrease production pressures thereby gradually allowing the client to reach his potential without causing severe damage physically or psychologically. Naturally, ongoing professional services are provided to the client during the time needed for adjustment to workshop production levels.

It should be understood that the workshop functions primarily on subcontracts obtained from industry which necessitates quality and quantity control in order to produce goods acceptable to the contractor. For this reason, many different operations are usually inherent in any average size workshop. Due to the variability of contracts in any given time, the client may function on many different types of assemblies or machine operations which, in turn, lends credence to future vocational plans. Of course, the types of operations found in any given workshop will vary in relation to its geographical setting which would dictate the types of factories and general industrial makeup of the area. For instance, the workshop in Cedar Rapids may be involved in furniture rebuilding and finishing; whereas, the workshop in Seattle, Washington, may be involved in lathe operations on missile parts. It behooves any workshop to obtain as many meaningful kinds of contracts as it is capable of providing equipment for in order to challenge and motivate the client toward obtaining vocational goals at the highest possible level.

It should be pointed out there that the old concept of obtaining repetitive and meaningless hand assembly operations are of little value to those retarded individuals who can be placed in industry. I wish to state, too, that there are greater variances in the functioning of the individual in the retarded range than there are in individuals functioning in the normal IQ ranges. If we look at the IQ spread in the retarded range of untestable to approximately 80 IQ, we find a range of 80 points; if we look at the IQ spread in the normal range of 90 to 125 we only find 35 points differential. Therefore, the expected ranges of behavior in regard to the mentally retarded are much more variable than that of the average, so called, "normal," person who also has the moral and socioeconomic pressures created by society.

For many years the informed worker in the field of mental retardation thought primarily of the service occupations as a vocational goal for the retarded. As proof to the contrary I need only to point to the statistics of the Nassau County Workshop which would indicate that the major proportion of clients placed in industry by this workshop fall into the unskilled or semi-skilled production worker category. Certainly the service occupations hold good placement opportunities for the mentally retarded and therefore the workshop should also contain training areas in such occupational titles as bus boy, counter man, dishwasher, porter, maintenance man, shipping and receiving clerk, and trucker's helper. All of these training areas should be an integral part of a workshop as it is in most factory settings.

The vocational training center and sheltered workshop should not attempt to train a retarded individual in a particular vocational skill unless that skill is easily marketable and can be incorporated with other similar job titles. The usual vocational training areas for the retarded which necessitate specific training procedures are most often found in the service occupations such as the use of buffing machines and cleaning equipment utilized by porters or custodial workers or the specific operations found in cafeteria work.

It is more to the point if the workshop creates a meaningful work activity program which can adjust the individual to the average demands placed on them by industry. These demands would include such things as coming to work on time, attention to job, relations with supervisors and co-workers, and other personality traits which make for a reliable and consistent worker. In most cases the retarded will not find employment in the semi-skilled and skilled occupations and for this reason dwelling on a specific marketable skill becomes an unrealistic and often disturbing goal for the retarded client.

Sheltered Employment

The previous comments are primarily geared toward training the retarded individual for placement. The second goal, but no less important, is to provide a place of employment for those who cannot meet competitive industrial standards. For want of a better term, this individual is known as "the terminal client." Persons designated as such may range in level depending completely on the policy of the workshop. Workshops with sufficient funding and space will tend toward encompassing a larger amount of lower-level retarded individuals who can function only on a minimal level. Those centers having limited funding will tend toward providing space for only those who can meet, or come close to, competitive standards. In either case, the workshop should only accommodate those individuals who have a "need to work." The definition of "need to work" can vary from need to feel useful to the simple need of getting up in the morning and traveling to a place of work like normal people. Of course, the monetary incentive also comes into play but appears to vary with the level of the individual. Regardless of the level of the retardate, the monetary compensation acts as a reward for a week of accomplishment, even if the individual is not able to read the amount.

Whether the goal is competitive employment or terminal employment, there is no doubt that the training phase is of major importance in order to provide some type of adjustment to the real work setting. This adjustment continues to take place for long periods of time contrary to the thinking of most and is borne out by the competitive placement of some individuals after a period of seven to ten years. In many cases the individual does reach a plateau beyond which he cannot be expected to function. Efforts must be made to enhance the potential of every individual in the workshop in the hope that some day he may become an integral part of the community which can pay off in large dividends. The dividends acquired by the community can take the form of the person placed in competitive employment who may also have been a former welfare recipient. Once placed in employment he then not only is removed from the welfare roles but becomes a taxpaying contributor and welcome member of society. This, we believe, is good business.

TRAINING PROGRAMS CURRENTLY AVAILABLE

Programs are carried out in the AHRC Vocational Training Center in Hempstead and at the Greenhouse and Boutique Shop established in the AHRC Educational Center at 189 Wheatley Road, Brookville (Glen Head), New York.

The Hempstead Center is a total facility having 26,000 sq. ft. at its disposal. The Brookville facility offers one classroom for the Boutique Shop, two large Greenhouses and eighteen acres of estate land for cultivation under the Greenhouse Program.

To facilitate transportation from the Hempstead to the Brookville Center and back, the Center operates one forty passenger school bus and one station wagon on a shuttle basis between Centers. In addition, shipment (delivery and pickup of subcontract material and finished products) is made possible through the operation of two large vans.

All of these transit facilities are used as training devices—the client transportation utilizes record-keepers, monitors and messengers; the vans require loaders, merchandise handlers and all around truckman's helpers.

Bench Assembly and Machine Operations specifically utilize subcontract work as training materials and a brief outline of typical work performed is listed. However, the remainder of the training programs are not specifically involved with subcontract work. Shipping, Receiving and Merchandise Handling utilize the raw materials and finished products of all the subcontracts delivered to and shipped from the Center. Office Practices training includes the use of some subcontract work if mimeographing or addressing is part of the subcontract, but usually Office Practices is considered part of the Center's own ongoing administrative functioning and trainees learn to perform required office services. The Tool Shop, Custodial and Janitorial Programs utilize the Center's own vital need for constant maintenance and repairs to provide training. The Cafeteria Program trains through providing food service to the trainee population and staff. The Child Care Program provides service to teachers and volunteers at our Brookville Educational Center for pre-school age children. There trainees are taught to help care for the personal needs of the mentally retarded young child. The Greenhouse Program offers training to develop proficiency in performing jobs associated with nursery, greenhouse, and landscaping operations.

Training titles listed under each program area are somewhat incomplete, and in some cases, a particular training title is listed under more than one program area. This results from the fact that only job titles which bear relation to the actual training area have been listed, whereas it is plausible to assume that someone trained in the cafeteria can easily become a competent bench worker and someone trained in the shipping area can become a cafeteria worker. Many instances of this kind of transfer of training ability can be noted in the Center, where trainees are moved from job to job as often as possible on the basis of their ability and the needs of production. This kind of transfer also frequently shows up in the kinds of job and success patterns of some of our trainees who enter competitive industry.

Bench Assembly

Simple, routine, repetitive, seated job requiring gross and/or fine manual dexterity skills. Trainees work alone and as part of an assembly line. The work performed usually consists of collecting and fitting together two or more pieces of an item and learning to make necessary visual and tactile discriminations among them. Sometimes requires use of small hand tools. Frequently involves appropriate use of specially designed jigs.

Equipment in area: foot and electric staple guns, stretching and carding racks, assorted jigs, electric screw setters.

Typical Subcontract Work

1. Hangar assembly: drive hole in wood hangar; insert hook and clinch; drive hook flush on bottom of hangar; fold filler around hangar; slide shirred sleeve over each end; staple in position; tie bow; pack two hangars to a box or insert two hangars to a cello sleeve.

2. Assembly of baby's bib set: insertion in specified position of four items taped in place onto card; insertion of hangar in polyethelene bag; placement of card with items in bag; transmitted to Shipping for carton packing.

Training titles: bench assembler, carder, packer, table worker, work distributor, assorter, folder.

Machine Operations

Varied in complexity. Some require simple, one-step operations. Others require a variety of operations to complete the machine cycle. In all cases, the operator learns daily machine maintenance requirements, the necessary machine skills, and appropriate safety measures.

Equipment in area: a variety of sealing equipment including eleven L Sealers; one motorized twenty foot conveyor, two shrink tunnels; two impulse sealers; constant heat sealers; plate sealers; semi-automatic cut off and bar sealers; semi-automatic, nongravity type cut off sealer; single jaw constant heat; foot-operated sealer; two impulse blister sealers; one hot plate blister sealer, one hot die blister sealer; three manually-operated floor drill presses; foot-operated grommeting and riveting machines; table saw, radial arm saw, band saw, sander, grinder, lathe, punch press.

Typical Subcontract Work

1. Aluminum wall plates: spot six holes in plate; drill to specifications; counterbore two holes; counter sink four holes; debur; transmit to Shipping.

2. Crystal lamp assembly and shrink packing: insertion of six nylon straps in a top and bottom ring; attachment of wires on large ring with pliers; hand insertion of fifteen plates; tying off; transmission to L Sealers and Shrink Tunnel; transmission to Shipping.

Training titles: machine operator, machinist helper, racker, table worker, work distributor, assorter, footpress operator, heat sealer, delivery boy, messenger.

Greenhouse Program

Landscaping, nursery, and florist training. Lawn and grounds maintenance. Planting, care, cutting and arranging of plants, vegetables and flowers. Preparation and arrangement of artificial floral products.

Typical Work Performed

1. The acreage on our Brookville estate is maintained through a training program which includes grass cutting and feeding; bush and hedge trimming and pruning; grounds raking; foundation and bed planting; weeding.

2. Individuals visiting the Brookville estate and other interested customers purchase potted house plants, vegetables, and cut flowers grown in our two greenhouses where training is provided in weeding, potting, and maintaining house plants. Also domestic vegetable gradens and flower beds are cultivated and maintained.

3. Training is also given in soil preparation, arrangements of cut flowers and plants, and of artificial flowers which are created to individual order.

Training titles: groundskeeper, landscape laborer, nursery laborer, brancher trainee (artificial flower manufacturing).

Shipping and Receiving

Transportation of raw materials or parts to assembly lines. Learns to use hand and mechanized lifts and conveyors. Makes cartons using a variety of sealing materials and stencils. Loads and unloads materials on trucks.

Equipment in area: two hydraulic lift trucks, two motorized fork lifts, three floor automatic conveyor belt system, ramps, hand trucks, electric tape shooters, stencil cutting machine, and gravity feed conveyors.

Training titles: stock man, wrapper, delivery man, retail receiving clerk, shipping room helper, vehicle loader, material distributor, counter, sorter, grocery checker, and truckers helper.

Merchandise Handling

Maintains storage areas by properly stacking and sorting raw materials and finished products as they are sent into or removed from area. Keeps simple inventory records of materials and finished products on hand. Counts and weights raw materials and finished products.

Equipment in area: utilizes all equipment in Shipping and Receiving; additionally utilizes a number of ratio counting and shadow graph scales.

Training titles: general office ratio clerk, mail clerk, marker, order filler, order picker, stock man, shipping room helper, counter, sorter, grocery checker.

Office Practices

Use of graphotype, addressograph, mailing and mimeograph machines. Copy typing, machine and hand collating and binding operations, simple attendance and payroll record keeping, monitor board, and receptionist training.

Equipment in area: PBX 507 Monitor Board, automatic mimeograph machine, automatic punch and binding equipment, building button telephone intercommunication system, mailing machine, typewriters, electric collator, foot pedal addressograph, graphotype machine.

Training titles: receptionist, duplicating machine operator, mail clerk, messenger, office clerk, ticketer, record copier, copy typist, file clerk, order filler, order picker, addressograph operator, graphotype plate maker, monitor board operator.

Tool Shop

Maintenance and repair of equipment in tool shop. Building maintenance routines including painting, basic carpentry, and machine maintenance. Production of jigs for use with subcontract materials.

Equipment in area: drill presses, hand drills, disc sanders, belt sanders, radial arm saw, bench saw, band saw, bench grinders lathe, air-operated hand tools.

Training titles: painter's helper, woodworker's helper, carpenter's helper, sander.

Custodial and Janitorial Services

Daily care and cleaning of floors, windows and offices using mops, pails, dusters and vacuum cleaners. Maintenance and supply of household areas.

Equipment in area: ringer pails, mops, industrial vacuum cleaner, household vacuum cleaner, equipment carts, standard industrial cleaning equipment.

Training titles: airplane cleaner, auto washer and polisher, shipyard laborer, porter, custodian's helper.

Cafeteria

Purchase, preparation, and service of food to large groups. Many of the trainees order their lunch from the cafeteria and the entire staff eats cafeteria-prepared lunches. Lunch is served in two shifts. In addition, the cafeteria serves a daily morning and afternoon snack and often prepares a completely separate luncheon for special visitors on special occasions. All of these foods are prepared and served by cafeteria trainees, some of whom also perform as cashiers. Maintenance and use of institutional kitchen equipment.

Equipment in area: hot food table, refrigerators, cold storage unit, jet spray dish dispensers, automatic electric coffee brewer, six-burner range and oven, griddles, electric fryers, dishwasher, utility carts, cash register and change dispenser.

Training titles: grocery checker, meat wrapper, nurses aide, busboy, cartman, dishwasher, kitchen helper, delivery man, supply room aide.

Child Care
Routines for care of patients and young children under professional supervision; food preparation and service on an individual basis. Essential homemaker activities.
Training titles: infant attendant, nurses aide, supply room aide.

FUNCTIONAL WORK CATEGORIES
In keeping with the Center's philosophy that specific job training for the mentally retarded must produce flexible work concepts readily translatable from one occupational area to another, the following work categories are listed by function performed. These categories conform to those found in the *Dictionary of Occupational Titles, vol. II,* "Occupational Classifications," 1965. A variety of job titles are subsumed under each function and each function is performed in a large number of industrial, service, and craft occupations. It is our experience that training offered in any one or a conjunction of the programs listed under each functional classification will produce a worker competent to perform that function.

Manipulating Occupations
Work performed: dextrous use of hands, hand tools or special devices to work, move, guide, or place objects or materials; works most frequently away from machine-oriented environment.
Requirements: eye-hand coordination; manual and finger dexterity; spatial and form perception; preference for working with hands; adaptation to routine.
Can receive training in: bench assembly, shipping and receiving merchandise handling, office practices, tool shop, cafeteria.

Sorting, Inspecting, Measuring and Related Occupations
Work performed: examining, measuring, weighing objects or materials for purpose of grading, sorting flaws or irregularities.
Requirements: ability and willingness to follow instructions to the letter; spatial and form discriminations; accuracy and attention to detail; finger and hand dexterity; eye-hand coordination; disposition to enjoy work of routine, repetitive and noncreative nature.

Can receive training in: bench assembly, machine operations, shipping and receiving, merchandise handling, cafeteria, office practices, tool shop.

Feeding, Offbearing, Handling Occupations

Work performed: inserting, throwing, dumping, placing, or removing materials from automatic machines or work areas of other workers.

Requirements: physical stamina; motor coordination; ability and willingness to follow instructions; hand and finger dexterity to position; feed or work with objects.

Can receive training in: machine operations, shipping and receiving, merchandise handling, greenhouse.

Tending Occupations

Work performed: starting, stopping, observing functioning of machines and equipment; workers change guides, adjust timers, temperature gauges, valves, pushing buttons, flipping switches and making other minor adjustments.

Requirements: inclination to work with machines and equipment; ability and willingness to follow instructions; adaptibility to routine; good attention span.

Can receive training in: machine operations, shipping and receiving, merchandise handling, cafeteria, office practices, custodial, tool shop, greenhouse.

Routine Checking and Recording Occupations

Work performed: checking, entering, posting verbal and numerical data on stocklists, ledgers, registers and other standardized records forms and performing related routine clerical duties.

Requirements: ability to learn and follow routine clerical procedures; verbal ability; clerical aptitude to keep accurate and legible records and perform bill, receipt, and invoice sorting tasks; temperament to perform repetitive work requiring constant and close attention to clerical details; numerical ability to perform simple arithmetic.

Can receive training in: office practices, merchandise handling.

Personal Service Occupations

Work performed: attending to personal consumption needs, clothing neatness, conveyance of luggage of individuals in public places.

Requirements: ability and willingness to take, understand, and follow instructions given by wide variety of people; courtesy, tact, and a desire to please others; manual dexterity.

Can receive training in: cafeteria, child care.

Messengers, Ushering Occupations

Work performed: carrying packages between destinations, relaying messages from one place to another, taking tickets, issuing programs, escorting people to seats in public places.

Requirements: ability to follow, understand, retain, and communicate information; ability to use public transportation, find street addresses; physical stamina; and in some cases willingness to wear a uniform.

Can receive training in: shipping and receiving, merchandise handling, cafeteria, child care, office practices.

Food Preparation and Food Service Occupations

Work performed: preparation of full meal or some specific portion of it in restaurants and other public or institutional food settings; serving individuals from a counter or at tables; cleaning and maintaining food supplies, eating areas, kitchen equipment, and utensils.

Requirements: ability to measure quantities; form and spatial perception to arrange food attractively; good eye-hand-foot coordination to use kitchen tools, appliances, and utensils; physical stamina; willingness to wear a uniform.

Can receive training in: cafeteria, child care.

Child and Adult Care Occupations

Work performed: assisting individuals totally or partially unable to care for themselves; transporting them in specially designed equipment; assistance in feeding them and caring for their personal hygiene.

Requirements: patience and sympathy for problems of others and courtesy and tact in dealing with them; stability under pressure; well-groomed personal appearance; good eye-hand-foot coordination.

Can receive training in: cafeteria, child care.

Artistic Restoration, Decoration and Related Work Occupations

Work performed: arranging, decorating, restoring, fashioning or similarly working objects and materials to produce an acceptable artistic effect or product.

Requirements: spatial perception to visualize three-dimensional forms and arrangements; visual acuity to observe differences in quality, form, color, texture; finger and hand dexterity; motor coordination; neatness and accuracy in handling materials; liking for aesthetic results.

Can receive training in: bench assembly, greenhouse, cafeteria, office practices.

Cropping, Farming, Gardening, Landscaping Occupations

Work performed: picking, tending, planting foods, vegetables, flowers, shrubs, bushes in a prescribed manner.

Requirements: interest in and liking for outdoor work; ability to comprehend and routinely carry out certain rules of plant life tending; eye-hand-finger coordination; ability to withstand temperature changes.

Can receive training in: greenhouse.

Typing and Related Recording Occupations

Work performed: recording or transmitting verbal or written material on to typewriter, tape perforator, Braille machine, graphotype.

Requirements: attentiveness to detail; motor coordination; finger dexterity; form perception; ability to take direction; adaptability to routine, repetitive work; and to make abrupt shifts from one job to another.

Can receive training in: office practices.

Switchboard and Receptionist Occupations

Work performed: operating telephone plugboard, monitor board, or button telephones to relay incoming, out-going, and internal phone calls; taking messages; supplying information.

Requirements: motor coordination; finger-eye-hand dexterity; good spatial and form perception; ability to deal tactfully and courteously with people; good hearing; and pleasant distinct speaking voice.

Can receive training in: office practices.

SUMMARY

Sheltered employment is provided to individual clients in all the program areas previously outlined. The workers participating in these workshops work side by side with those being trained for competitive employment. In many instances sheltered workers provide the most effective leadership available to new trainees. They are experienced "old hands" who are able to guide new trainees through the difficult maze of learning who is responsible for what and through the social initiation process met in the Center. Sheltered workers also form the hard core of competent workers who can always be relied upon to meet production schedules in the assembly and machine subcontract areas.

In addition, the Boutique Shop on our grounds in Brookville provides sheltered employment only to a number of trainees who are productive workers but can not withstand the environmental stresses inherent in the factory atmosphere prevailing in Hempstead. These workers are engaged in producing individual orders of novelty gift items and party goods.

PART II
The Brain Injured

Chapter 7

Teaching the Brain-Injured Child—Elementary Level

ELEANOR ZOUEFF

INTRODUCTION

This class at the present time contains children aged seven through eleven with neurological impairments. These children all show evidence of perceptual and/or behavior problems which have created academic retardation and social maladjustment. For these reasons they could not be maintained in a regular classroom. The special class size is small, since most instruction is individual, and there must be a more permissive atmosphere. The child is not competing with his group and in most cases he gradually becomes more relaxed and less hyperactive. The objective of the brain-injured class is to help the child socially and academically to the extent that he may eventually return to the regular classroom.

The program is a structured one since the child requires a feeling of security and needs to develop a sense of organization. He is first trained in the areas of perception before any academic learning can take place. As he becomes more competent in such areas as visual, auditory, tactile, body-image, space orientation, laterality, and figure-ground perception, he then begins the academic work on the level which he easily comprehends and which will not cause him to become frustrated. Then he proceeds at his own rate of speed from level to level. Group work is carried on for such subjects as writing, science, English, and social studies. The children go out to have gym as a group once a week, music once a week, art once a week, and individual and group speech correction twice each week.

191

TABLE 19
PERCEPTION TRAINING[1]

Units	Activities	Materials
I. Visual Perception Training		
A. Visual memory training		
1. matching	Matching shapes, designs Draw shapes, numbers, designs on board or paper after looking at teacher's copy	Visual perception dittos (standardized and teacher-made
2. visual memory techniques	Object Removal Game—teacher place several objects on a table; child looks, closes eyes; teacher removes an object and child opens eyes and tells which was removed then he will try to name all objects with back turned to the table.	slides from supervisor's office on fairy tales, rhyming, etc. put together puzzles "Look and Learn" lotto game play store card game Bolts and Nuts Game Farm Lotto
3. eye-training exercises	Eye-training exercises—child holds pencil at arms length and follows the eraser end of his pencil as he moves it from right to left, vice versa, up down and in large circle, always keeping eyes on eraser; then same procedure with one eye closed, then the other eye closed. This may be done by first moving the head as eyes follow target, then at another time without moving the head.	"Rig-A-Jig" construction Game "Match Me" card game teacher-prepared materials—(patterns to color, stick and bead designs, etc.)

[1] Most children who have been diagnosed brain injured evidence problems in the perceptual area. Major areas for perceptual training include: auditory and visual relationships; body imagery; and gross and fine motor activity.

TABLE 19 (*Continued*)
PERCEPTION TRAINING[1]

Units	Activities	Materials
4. visual perception	Copy parquetry block designs, colored cube designs and pegboard patterns from teacher's design; String beads following teacher's bead pattern; child sorts shapes, colors, sizes of cardboard or felt forms, beads, etc.	beads and string parquetry blocks
5. gross motor coordination	Child has much practice in coloring, cutting and pasting large pictures which teacher has made on ditto; reproduce stick patterns; sorting colors, shapes, objects.	sticks and paper patterns
	Child traces large model of various designs at the blackboard using whole arm (such as large circles, figure 8) then with chalk in both hands, he makes large circles both going in same direction, then in reverse direction with both hands, then with both hands going in opposite directions forming the two circles.	
	Creeping races; cross pattern walking; balance board; pushups; scissors jump; paint large board in various color squares and children jump in colored areas with alternate feet as directed.	

TABLE 19 (Continued)
PERCEPTION TRAINING[1]

Units	Activities	Materials
II. Auditory Perception Training A. Auditory memory training	Child repeats numbers in sequence following teacher; child repeats nonsense syllables; child repeats unrelated words; child listens, then repeats three or four numbers backwards and/or forward.	"Let's Listen" Album of Sounds (Scott Foresman Company)
	Teacher gives child two or three oral directions—child repeats them then carries them out. "Listen to these numbers then tell me the largest—2, 4, 7, 5, 9." Same procedure for smallest, next to last. (All with different numbers.)	Records: "What Makes Rain?" "What Is a Star?" (Decca) Plus records on fairy tales, etc. found in supervisor's office and also classroom records
	Teacher claps with back to class, then child claps same number times. Teacher bounce a ball with back to class; then ask a child to imitate the bouncing. Use same procedure with beating a small drum or blowing a whistle. Teacher plays a note on piano and asks if its *high* or *low*. Teacher calls name of an animal. Children listen to a record played by teacher, then answer questions about it or dramatize it. "Raise your hand when you hear something that could not happen": a dog singing a song, a book reading a story, a boy play-	fairy tales in books "An Introduction to Sound" "A Method For Teaching" (Both by Educational Records

TABLE 19 *(Continued)*
PERCEPTION TRAINING[1]

Units	Activities	Materials
	ing ball, etc. With back to class, teacher may do any of the following and ask child to tell what it is: tear a paper, tap with a pencil on wood or metal, jingle coins, blow a whistle, cough, bounce a ball, close a door, etc. Ask children to tell you what they heard on the way to school (e.g., make the sound of a cat feeling sad, make the sound of a dog who is excited, make a cow sound angry, etc.) *Following directions:* teacher says, "At the board draw a circle, put an X inside it, draw a box next to it and make three lines under it", etc. or this may be done by the group at their desks using paper, pencils or crayons.	
	Rhyming: teacher says, "Run, run and we'll have ——." Children call out the word that rhymes. Make any rhymes you may wish.	
	Guessing game: One child may describe another pupil's appearance (hair, eyes, clothing when the child described recognizes himself he is "It."	

TABLE 19 (*Continued*)
PERCEPTION TRAINING[1]

Units	Activities	Materials
III. Tactile Perception Training	Child feels of cardboard shapes which teacher hands him one by one (behind his back) and he identifies—circle, square, etc. Same procedure with various objects (pencil, etc.) After child feels of each shape, he goes to the board and draws it without looking at it. (circle, square, etc.).	teacher-prepared materials: cardboards shapes made of felt materials brought from home for tactile stimulation
	As child has hands behind him, give him a piece of cotton, wood, sandpaper, etc. and ask him how it feels. Give child a book or heavy object, then a feather, pencil or light object; ask which is heavier—lighter.	
	Play guessing game (what is hard, soft, sticky, furry, etc.).	materials brought from home and materials used in classroom
IV. Taste Perception Training	Give small samples of fruits, sugar, chocolate for child to taste with his eyes closed. See which child can identify the largest number.	
	Guessing game—"I am thinking of something that tastes," sour, sweet, bitter, salty, etc.	

TABLE 19 (*Continued*)
PERCEPTION TRAINING[1]

| V. Spatial Relations | Guessing game: "I see something *over* the door. I see something *under* your desk, *next* to James, *on* my desk, *by* the reading table, etc. Children guess each one as teacher says them.

Following directions: Teacher says, "Put your pencil *on* your desk. Put your paper *under* your desk, stand *behind* your chair, etc." Then have each child, one at a time listen, then carry out, "Go to the back of the room—on the way, go *around* Danny's desk, walk *over* Joyce's chair, crawl *under* the table, then stand by the sink." These directions may be given in fewer actions at first, then increase. Take a ball and basket. Give a child directions for putting the ball *in* the basket, *under* it, take it *out*, put it *next* to basket, etc. | *The Aphasic Child*
Hortense Barry
The Listening Walk
Paul Showers (Crowell Pub.)
Teaching Method for Brain Injured and Hyperactive Children William Cruikshank, et al. (Syracuse University Press)
The Exceptional Child James Magary and John Eichorn, Eds. (Holt Rinehart Pub.)
Psychopathology and Education of Brain-Injured Children
A. A. Strauss
(Grune and Stratton Pub.) |

TABLE 20
READING

Units	Activities	Materials
I. Reading Readiness mental age of six years or more	I. Name colors, sort into groups	teacher-prepared material such as cardboard circles, squares, triangles, etc.
	Sort forms of different sizes and colors	dittos for matching, differences, etc.
	Reproduce a pattern from a model	letters and pictures cut from old workbooks
	Sort letters according to shape	plastic letters
	Match pictures	letters made from cardboard
	Imitate sounds	
	Imitate actions	Filmstrips:
	Repeat sentences orally	*Phonetic Skills—Basic Reading Program*
	Track a pattern from left to right	(Scott Foresman)
	Practice showing left ear, right ear (hand, foot, etc.)	records
	Use pocket chart for matching shapes, colors	
	Match pictures starting with the same sound	
	Be able to tell a story orally by looking at a series of pictures	
	Give opposites of familiar words	
	Look at three pictures and tell what will happen next	

TABLE 20 *(Continued)*
READING

Units	Activities	Materials
II. Pre-primer Level (after standardized test "Before We Read" is given)	II. Ear training in auditory discrimination of initial sounds and final consonants	workbooks may be cut up for picture matching, sequence, etc.
	Experience charts for left-right training	"Sounds for Young Readers" — Volume I, II (records) Classroom Materials, Inc. Great Neck, N. Y.
	Visual discrimination—match pictures, abstract geometric forms, letter groups	The group uses the Scott-Foreman readers:
	Listen and supply a missing word as child listens to a sentence or while looking at a picture	*We Look and See* *We Come and Go* *We Work and Play*
	Arrange several pictures in sequence	with accompanying workbooks
	Tell the main idea in a story or paragraph read by teacher	"Match Me"—card game
	Make scrapbooks of pictures that start with the same sounds (children bring in old magazines for cutting)	"Animal Rummy" card game Sequees Games
III. Primer Level A. first reader	III. Use teacher-made charts for initial and final sounds. Recognize and tell the sound and name of initial consonants when teacher reads a word then write the letter. Same procedure for final consonants. Recognize	prepared charts by teacher for initial and final sounds Ideal School Supply Charts for phonic training

TABLE 20 (*Continued*)
READING

Units	Activities	Materials
	when heard the speech consonants (ch sh wh th) consonant blends (gr, st, sw, cl, sk, sh, sp, br, gl, fl, pl, fr, etc.)	Scott-Foresman's Basal books and workbooks: *Fun with Dick and Jane* *Fun with Our Friends* *Good Times with Our Friends* *Our New Friends* *More Fun with Our Friends* Filmstrip: *Phonetic Skills* *Basic Reading Program* (Scott-Foresman)
	Recognize, when heard, the endings on root words (s, ing, ed)	
	Make families orally and written from such phonograms as—an, at, ell, ad, ell, all, ack	
	Play rhyming game: clap or stand when child hears a word that rhymes	
B. Second reader	Develop such skills as *making judgments*, substitution of initial consonants, as bat, cat, fat and substitution of final consonants, as, bat, bad, ban; *extending interpretation*, as "What other story did you read where a boy also had a secret?" etc.; *forming visual images*—"Close your eyes and try to see a telephone, a little brown squirrel, a red barn, etc." Teacher may read a poem which will add to the enjoyment of a particular story or also appropriate songs.	*New Friends and Neighbors* (Workbook) *Time for Poetry* (Scott-Foresman) *New Music Horizons* (Ginn)

TABLE 20 (*Continued*)
READING

Units	Activities	Materials
	Vowel sounds also to be studied	
	Main idea—children may draw and color a picture which portrays what the story was about.	
	Anticipating outcomes—after a part of the story has been read, ask children: "What do you think Billy will do to solve his problem?" or "Why do you think Jack wanted to go to Grandmother's?"	

[*Note:* Continue with each reading level according to individual needs and ability.]

TABLE 21
ARITHMETIC²

Units	Activities	Materials
I. Number Readiness		
A. Number concepts through 10	Use concrete objects for learning number concepts through 10 (abacus, blocks, beads, buttons, etc.)	blocks
1. enumeration (one to one correspondence between two sets of things)	Teacher-child games such as "Show me the group of blocks with 3 in it" or "Show me a set of beads with 5 in it" or "Which two sets have the same number of beads or blocks," etc.	beads
2. identification (in groups of colored blocks or beads)	"Give 5 red beads to me"	buttons
3. recognition	"Look at these two sets of blocks—which has more? less?" and how many more in this set or how many less in this?"	lotto game—bingo game
4. comparison		shapes of felt
		flannelboard
		dominos
		Catherine Stern wooden set of materials
		A Teaching Method For Brain-Injured and Hyperactive Children
		William Cruikshank, et. al. (Syracuse University Press)

² Many brain-injured children cannot think abstractly; therefore it is evident that number work will represent a problem to them. A child first coming into the elementary class from kindergarten works and manipulates devices to learn skill in nesting blocks, fitting shapes into the correct grooves, copying a master pattern with sticks, parquetry blocks, pegboards, fitting puzzles together, working with Montessori materials to learn number sizes and shapes, stringing beads to imitate a model, and through the Catherine Stern wooden object set to learn number sequence and the number concepts. In other words, the child learns through concrete materials first, before he can go to a more abstract level of learning. From here, he progresses to being able to work out examples and problems copied from the board and through workbooks on his present object or number of objects so that the child can see and feel them. The children are also introduced to the new modern math on a primer level using such vocabulary as "greater than," "equivalent," "now equivalent sets," "less than," and adding and subtracting horizontally as well as vertically. Multiplication and division are then introduced to the children who are ready for it through the new method of math learning. Most of these children enjoy the arithmetic periods and work well independently when they understand what is to be done.

TABLE 21 (*Continued*)
ARITHMETIC

Units	Activities	Materials
	Play lotto and bingo games to reinforce recognition of numbers 1-10	"Structured Arithmetic Set" Catherine Stern (Houghton Mifflin)
5. grouping (to see objects in a set without counting)	"Can you tell me how many beads are in this set? (00) (000) (00) (000) etc.	
	The child first constructs the number series (counting) by inserting the block sticks into the correct grooves in the pattern board. As he continues to work with this material and with guidance from the teacher, he will learn such concepts as "shorter," "longer," "more," "less," then later he can see what addition and subtraction mean through examining the number of blocks as compared with that of another group.	
	Montessori materials: materials used for sensory training through handling various kinds of simple objects such as graded cylinder sets with knobs for dimension and depth concept, geometric problem boards for developing shape and form concept through inserting shapes	Montessori materials

TABLE 21 (*Continued*)
ARITHMETIC

Units	Activities	Materials
	into the pattern board, tracing them on paper and guessing games with closed eyes.	teacher-prepared dittos number charts Cartherine Stern materials flannelboard and cut-outs

II. First Level Concepts
A. Count and write to 100
  1. write by 2's to 50
  2. write by 5's to 100
  3. write by 10's to 100
  4. write numbers 1-100 as dictated
B. Recognize nickel, cent, dime
C. Correlate number words
	Games, songs, drawings to further the understanding of number progression and comparison (e.g. play bowling game and bean bag game: one child keeps score, add each score to determine winners)	*Mathematics Made Meaningful Volume I* (for K-2) with activities and games for developing concepts of counting, adding, subtracting, etc.
		teacher-made flannel cutouts
		buttons, beads, cardboard discs

D. 1-10 with figure
E. Number Concepts:
  1. ability to count forward and backward 1-10
  2. knowledge of preceding or succeeding number
  3. comparative sense (more, less, same)
	Using the Catherine Stern materials for developing concept of number progression, comparative thinking etc (as child fits the blocks into the correct grooves he sees which block is longer, shorter, has how many more grooved sections etc.)	Catherine Stern materials
		Montessori materials
		"Combinations are Fun"
		Kenworthy game

4. grouping of sets
    $5 = 2+3$ or $4+1$ or $3+2$, etc.
  5. horizontal recording of combinations in this order:
    00 and 0 are 000
    2 and 1 are 3
    $2 + 1 = 3$
	Reproduce pegboard patterns which involve counting and correct placing of single and groups of pegs
	Work with teacher individually on these concepts	

TABLE 21 (*Continued*)
ARITHMETIC

Units	Activities	Materials
6. vertical Recording of combinations $\begin{array}{r} X \\ XX \\ \hline XXX \end{array}$ and $\begin{array}{r} 2 \\ +1 \\ \hline 3 \end{array}$	Play games on flannelboard with horizontal and vertical sets in addition Child may make his own set of addition flash cards for practice in school and at home	"Combination Balance" game
7. combination tables of addition first understood then drilled for instant recall $\begin{array}{r} 1 \\ +1 \\ \hline \end{array}$ $\begin{array}{r} 1 \\ +2 \\ \hline \end{array} \quad \begin{array}{r} 2 \\ +1 \\ \hline \end{array}$ $\begin{array}{r} 1 \\ +3 \\ \hline \end{array} \quad \begin{array}{r} 3 \\ +1 \\ \hline \end{array} \quad \begin{array}{r} 2 \\ +2 \\ \hline \end{array}$	Montessori materials used for actual handling of shapes and sizes of wooden objects and for judging depth, circumference, etc.	
III. Second Level Concepts		
A. Continue number tables in addition through $5 + 5$, $6 + 4$, $9 + 1$, $7 + 3$ and $8 + 2$	Child will make own set of addition flash cards for school and home practice Play store: one child is grocery clerk, another buys with a dime or nickel and receives change	real coins, articles for toy store real or drawn on board child-made stamps, real cookies fraction game: "Fractions are Easy as Pie"
B. Know coin values of penny, nickel, dime, quarter as 1¢, 5¢, 10¢, 25¢	Play post office, buy stamps use real coins	pint and quart cardboard containers

TABLE 21 (Continued)
ARITHMETIC

Units	Activities	Materials
C. Make change from a nickel and a dime	Teacher may divide cookies into fractions to see which piece is smallest, largest	large clock face small individual clock faces rulers, yardstick
D. Understand meaning of fractions $\frac{1}{2}$, $\frac{1}{3}$, $\frac{1}{4}$	Children may make and keep their own weather calendars	
E. Know and read days of week, months, seasons	Children measure with actual quart and pint containers and measure objects with foot ruler and yardstick	
F. Time (hour—$\frac{1}{2}$ hour)		
G. Measures (pint, quart, foot, yard)		

TABLE 22
SOCIAL STUDIES

Units	Activities	Materials
I. Family Life A. Members (adults, children, pets) B. Needs of family 1. food 2. shelter 3. clothing (kinds, how it changes with the seasons) 4. types of work of family members C. Celebrating holidays (national)	I. Cut pictures from old magazines to show family members at work or recreation; make large poster with these. Children may make own scrapbooks of "My Family." Children may make various kinds of rooms in a house from cardboard boxes. Class makes original cards for their family at holiday times.	discarded magazines *Seven Little Postmen* (Golden Books) *Our Family*—(Benefic Press) *At Home* (Scott Foresman) *Living in Our Time* Allyn Bacon
II. Community Helpers—Who are They? A. Policeman, fireman, milkman, doctor nurse, trashman, grocer B. Importance to community C. Duties of each one D. How does their work help your family and the community?	II. Children may make a large mural of community helpers, group may make own booklets titled "Our Community Helpers," children find out news from newspaper read to them by parents and then tell it to the class.	*Our Friendly Helpers* Hoffman and Hofflefinger (Melmont Publ.) filmstrips available in supervisor's office to make these concepts more real and understandable *The True Book of Policemen and Firemen*—Irene Miner (Childrens Press) *I Want To Be a Fireman* (Childrens Press)
III. News of Town and World (discussed weekly)	III. Keep a large bulletin board with current events and pictures brought by children from home.	
IV. Modern Transportation A. Land—car, bus, track, train B. Sea—ships, cargo, passenger C. Air—types of planes	IV. Read to class about various types of transportation, play records, children make a transportation mural	*The True Book of Cars and Trucks*

TABLE 23
SCIENCE

Units	Activities	Materials
I. *Our Earth*		
A. Sky	Booklets may be made by children titled "The Sky"	*We Read About Series* (Gardner Publ.)
1. sun	Show sky map to point out familiar constellations. Children may draw free hand sky charts showing these and also charts with the nine planets. Children may memorize planets in their distance from the sun.	*Science for Children K-3* University of N. Y. State Bureau of Elementary Curriculum
2. moon		*Exploring Science I* Allyn Bacon
3. planets		filmstrips available in the supervisor's office to further these concepts of scientific information
4. constellations		
5. day and night		
B. Air and space	Children make scrapbooks of things that give light and heat	*All Around Us* (Scott Foresman)
C. Weather	Make simple weather chart	Records (Decca): "What Makes Rain?"
1. changes	Children may put up weather symbols each day	"Wht Is a Star?"
2. effects		"What Is the Moon?"
3. precipitation	Experiments to show evaporation of water (water in dish on radiator or watch water in a puddle)	globe, flashlight for day-night experiment balls—various sizes
D. Soil	Experiment with globe to show night and day	*Winter Is Here, Spring Is Here, Summer Is Here, Autumn is Here*—Bertha Parker (Row Peterson & Co.)
1. composition	Booklets of our class experiments kept by each child	*What Is Series* (Benefic Press)
2. rocks		
3. trees common to our area	Booklets made by each child to show how our clothing changes with the seasons	
E. Seasons		
1. characteristics	Individual booklets with stories, poems, and drawings about the seasons	
2. clothing	Class made mural with healthful foods for each meal	
3. foods		

TABLE 24
LANGUAGE ARTS³

Units	Activities	Materials
I. Spelling		
A. *Readiness first level*	A. Games, songs	filmstrips (hearing sounds in words, letters which work together, consonant sound)
1. listening to initial consonants for same sounds in words, then listen and recognize final consonants in various words	Nursery rhymes for sound and rhyme concepts	teacher-made sound charts
	Children make scrapbooks of pictures brought from home magazines illustrating the various initial consonants, final consonants	large chart (portable) of sounds Ideal School Supply Co.
2. rhyming—children hear and recognize rhyming words	Card game with matching sounds	Initial consonant
	Teacher plays game with children as they clap or stand when hearing a certain initial consonant or rhyme	Final consonant rhymes
3. learn basic sight word vocabulary for spelling common, frequently used words for written communication	Children keep individual notebooks with words commonly used in daily written work	dittos for children to work individually or as a group
		"My Red Puzzle" I. (for learning a sight vocabulary)
	I. Note: (These are all done according to the child's own level and ability)	

³ This part of our curriculum may be called the "Communicative" Arts. It is an extremely important area. Not all normal children have the innate ability to listen. Children with brain injury will often need to be taught the essential skill of listening. Special periods for listening are introduced for this reason. The equally important skill of oral communication with others is developed. Children enjoy talking but not all of them are able to structure a correct sentence or to enunciate clearly. A speech therapist may have to give them help and this is done twice each week, both individually and then with the group. Handwriting is introduced when the child has a satisfactory sight vocabulary and it is first taught through the word "family" or phonetic method. Later, sentences are dictated when a sufficient number of words have been learned. Since we all spend at least three-fourths of our time in communication, this program is a continuing one from day to day.

TABLE 24 (Continued)
LANGUAGE ARTS

Units	Activities	Materials
B. Spelling second level	B. Continue as above with more difficult words	"Goals in Spelling" I.
II. English		
A. Spoken (oral)	Child talks before the group on home activities, experiences, T.V. programs	*The Child and His Curriculum* J. M. Lee (Appleton-Century)
1. conversation and discussion	Child-led discussions of manners, school conduct, etc.	Records for "Children With Special Needs" Creative Playthings Inc. Cranbury, N. J.
2. announcements	Daily newspaper	
3. informal telling of jokes and riddles		
4. dramatizations (flannelboard and puppet plays)		
B. Written	II. Children write invitations to imaginary activities, thank-you letters, get well letters, short imaginary stories	
1. letters		
2. experience stories	Chart stories	
3. creative writing		
4. correct use of pronouns, verbs		
C. Listening (this is a learned skill)	III. Teacher reads poems and stories for enjoyment and for factual questions, getting main idea, sequence, etc.	fairy tale records *Time for Poetry* (Scott Foresman)
1. to another child	Play records with various sounds, fairy tales, etc., then have a group discussion or individual questions	*A Teaching Method for Brain-Injured Children* William Cruikshank (Syracuse Univ. Press)
2. to the teacher	Children make story booklets, poem booklets of materials copied from teacher's work	
3. to records	Daily or weekly class newspaper with events of our class and our school	

TABLE 24 *(Continued)*
LANGUAGE ARTS

Units	Activities	Materials
III. Writing (Sequence) A. Manuscript 1. small letters i t x v w z k y o c a d g j f s q u r n m h b p	A. Introduce letters as follows: 1. stickletters—these are introduced first as they require the least co-ordination and children with perceptual difficulties can more easily see how they are kept within the lines of the writing paper. 2. circle letters 3. combined forms 4. reversed circle letters The circle letters are introduced to a child when he has developed greater coordination and muscular control and when he can better keep within the lines. In forming circle letters, the teacher must emphasize that the circle starts below the line and goes up to touch the line. This forms a basis for carry over to script. Then reverse circle letters are introduced.	blackboard for children to practice teachers copy of letters primary grade writing paper, large penmanship primary pencils
2. capital letters a. stick letters L E T I H N V M Y W A X Z K	Introduce the capital letters in a similar sequence starting with the stick-shaped letters. Then proceed to the circle letters, arc letters, and finally to the combined arc and line letters. Children may learn the formation of these letters at the blackboard first in	

TABLE 24 (*Continued*)
LANGUAGE ARTS

Units	Activities	Materials
b. Circle letters O Q C G D P R B (arc and straight lines) J U S (arc letters)	large sizes between straight lines, then they may transfer to the primary lined paper and pencils. For children having difficulty, one part of a letter may be made in a certain colored pencil (e.g. green) the remaining part in (e.g red).	Univ. of N. Y. State Elem. Curriculum 1960
B. Cursive writing	B. Make the change over from manuscript when letters are formed and spaced well and before the habit of manuscript writing has been too firmly fixed to make a smooth change. Steps to be taken: 1. children are taught to slant their papers 2. teach those cursive letters first that differ from manuscript, as b e f h r s 3. teach children to join the letters, use blackboard to illustrate, then children may come to the board and trace the teacher's model 4. much practice is important 5. simple sentences are written 6. supervise a writing period each day 7. encourage and illustrate the combined movements of fingers, hand, arm	primary pencils *Children's Experiences in Handwriting* V. E. Herrick (Prentice-Hall)

Chapter 8

Teaching the Brain-Injured Child— Junior High School Level

PHILOMENA SINAGRA

FOREWORD

This program has been devised to meet the needs of those pupils of normal intellectual potential beween the ages of twelve and fifteen who have been diagnosed as neurologically impaired with resulting learning disabilities, behavioral problems, or both.

Behavioral problems arise as a result of lack of impulse control and manifest themselves in extreme distractability, hyperactivity, short attention span, and a generally disorganized pattern of functioning in all situations both behaviorally and academically.

Learning disabilities are primarily due to dysfunctions of the visual, auditory, or tactual areas of perception which do not permit the pupil to gain meaningful or organized significance from the sensations which he receives. The manifestations of perceptual disturbances are seen in difficulties with eye-hand coordination, figure-ground perception, form constancy, laterality and directionality, spatial relationships, body image, and concept of self. If there is motor involvement as well, the pupil may have further problems with speech, muscular coordination, and body control.

The effects of these problems on the emotional development of these pupils can not be overlooked. Through the years, because of their inability to perform appropriately in the areas of behavior and academics, they have experienced failure and rejection in the home, the school, and the community. Because their emotional

213

needs have been poorly met, they have developed feelings of inadequacy and unworthiness.

This program holds as its primary objective meeting the needs of its pupils in any or all areas of development where difficulties may exist—socially, academically, or emotionally—by promoting and providing opportunities whereby each may develop to his fullest potential and whereby each may achieve the realization of self-worth that is essential to his taking a place as a productive member of our adult society.

WHY A REGULAR JUNIOR HIGH SETTING

The Nature and Needs of Adolescence as Met by the Junior High

The uniqueness of this particular program is that it was designed to operate in a regular junior high school building and to function within the framework of a regular junior high schedule. In 1964, for the first time, a junior high school class of brain-injured pupils was established. This was not by chance but by design.

Adolescence is known to be a critical time in the developmental process of all youngsters. It is characteristically a time when aspirations and ideals take root; a time when social behavior and attitudes develop. It is also a time when adult values are tested and accepted or rejected; a time when greater importance is placed upon peer-group acceptance and status; a time when independence from parental ties is strived for but where the security of an understanding adult is sought. Such concepts as "citizenship," "government," "culture," and "ethics" evolve and begin to take concrete form. The neo-adult is shaping his image into the adult he will soon become—but during the process his emotional balance is somewhat chaotic.

The junior high school by its very nature provides for those experiences and opportunities which allow for these concepts to grow and shape in the proper direction. There is no doubt that deprivation of opportunities to experience interrelationships with the society of other adolescents may seriously hamper if not permanently distort the values and concepts we look for in mature, well-adjusted adults. Brain-injured children often suffer from social and emotional deprivation because of limited opportunities to participate in regular and extra-curricular school activities. Additionally, lack of acceptance or lack of ability to participate in out-of-school and neighborhood activities can cause further deprivation; this becomes especially true when the brain-injured pupil is removed from the community or is placed in a class operated as a self-contained entity. Thus, the experiences that the junior high can offer become essential! They represent a "last chance," so to speak, for him to gain those concepts necessary to enter the world of adults as a self-sufficing, self-respecting individual.

It must be remembered that although these students are considered handicapped because of learning disabilities and/or behavioral difficulties that make it necessary for them to be provided special teaching methods, in many areas they may function at average or even above average levels. Thus, some of these pupils have major reading problems but verbalize exceptionally well; some function well in academic areas but find it difficult to communicate orally or to relate well to others. We also find that some cannot function academically except on very low levels but have talents in mechanical, artistic, or musical pursuits. While some are physically inept, others possess excellent athletic abilities. Some are impulsive and aggressive and others are shy or relatively withdrawn. *All*, however, have areas wherein they can function in some aspect of regular school situations.

It is in these areas of average functioning that we offer the brain-injured child an alternative to the limited, depriving environment of the special class situation and into the environment of the regular junior high with its broader, richer experiential opportunities. If provided with experiences necessary to develop more fully, the brain-injured pupil has a better chance to eventually disassociate himself from the atypical world of the handicapped and to integrate more readily into the world of the useful, productive citizenry. Conversely, peer groups, the community, and soviety in general are also more ready to accept the brain-injured young adult who has already proven himself capable of living and functioning successfully among them. The stigma attached to the awesome label "brain injured" (with the even more awesome inferences it often conjures) can be somewhat minimized.

How the Opportunities Provided in a Regular Junior High
Are Utilized

The common denominator for all the pupils in this class is neurological impairment with normal intelligent potential. However, these pupils come with varied educational backgrounds and even more varied levels of academic achievement. Therefore, before placement into areas of the regular junior high can be made, each pupil must be evaluated in terms of his individual progress in each academic area as well as in his ability to function behaviorally in a regular classroom situation. To better determine the pupil's possible integration into regular junior high areas, his folder should contain records of previous school and grade placements, health records, teacher reports, achievement test results, and psychological testing data; all must be thoroughly studied. Also, the special class teacher will have to administer diagnostic tests to determine current grade levels in academic skill areas and to observe his ability to function for a sustained period of time without becoming either disruptive or distracted. This evaluation is an ongoing process which continues throughout the year and is forever changing as the child develops and changes.

Each child begins as a seventh grade pupil and attends music, art, and gym classes with other members of the regular seventh grade student body. Integration begins at this level. When a student has demonstrated his ability to function reasonably well for a period of about 40-45 minutes and where it is felt that he can successfully cope with the academic and social demands of a given area, he is then recommended for placement in a regular class by the special class teacher.

Placement is determined through the cooperative efforts of the principal, the coordinator of special education, and the guidance department who work with the special class teacher in making the best possible placement in terms of teacher selection, class size, etc. They also help arrange for integration of the group as a whole into regular physical education, music, art, and industrial arts classes as well as for participation in the regular lunchroom procedure.

If any pupil so placed proves unable to function acceptably in any one area, he can then be returned to the self-contained special classroom situation of his homeroom. Since this constitutes a failure on the part of the student in his own eyes, it is most important that no child be integrated until there is reasonable assurance of his success in that area.

Once a pupil has been placed in a regular school area, the special class teacher then works with the regular class teacher to explain the pupil's particular problems and to help both the teacher and pupil in making the placement a successful one.

The speech department is called upon to provide weekly speech improvement classes for the group as whole and individual or small group speech correction classes wherever necessary. This is a very important service to this class as some pupils have minimal cerebral palsy with concomitant speech problems while others may have language disorders which result in poor ability to verbalize.

The physical education department provides by far one of the most important services available to this program. A chain is as strong as its weakest link, meaning here that the total development of the child must be recognized as crucial to his sucess in any one area of development. Brain-injured pupils very frequently display poor body image and control. This is due to perceptual dysfunctions directly to lesions in the perceptual areas of the brain. Where this is the case, the sensory stimuli that the brain receives become disstorted and the child experiences errors in judgment of size, shape, distance, direction, etc. This impaired perceptual functioning creates problems in spatial relationships, laterality, and directionality. These problems are very often at the root of learning disabilities or academic failures. Therefore, the gym class, which, through its regular activities, permits the child to test his body and its extremities, to learn where he begins and ends, and to come to realize he can be master of his movements, is in reality also developing the perceptual abilities of the child and feeding directly into the academic learning prerequisites which demand the body know spatial relationships, laterality, and directionality. The physical education department has accepted the pupils of this class into their regular classes with no serious problems reported.

The music department provides participation in seventh and

eight grade general music classes for all the students of this class. They will also accept into band or orchestra any pupil who plays a musical instrument. Chorus will be open to pupils of eighth or ninth grade levels who qualify.

Industrial arts is offered for one half a year in both seventh and eighth grades to all the special class pupils where they have an opportunity to develop and explore manual skills. They work with ceramics, metal, and glass. In ninth grade, they can choose industrial arts as an elective subject. Woodworking, electrical design, metal work, and general tool experiences are offered in the industrial arts shop.

Art classes show individual differences greatly. Some children are very artistic and display a good sense of perspective and color form while others manifest their perceptual difficulties in their inability to draw, color within lines, or to cut on a line. However, pupils usually enjoy art classes and participate well. In ninth grade, those who have found themselves to be successful in art classes, may choose basic art as an elective.

Co-curricular and extra-curricular activities are also open to the students who are interested. One boy who feels inadequate physically because of cerebral palsy and thus shies away from participating in after-school sports has found a new world for himself as a library helper and a member of the library council. He speaks of someday working as a library assistant. Two other class members are also valued as library council members and are genuinely sought after for their assistance. This experience, providing a feeling of worthiness and usefulness, is invaluable to the total development of the pupils and is for some their first such experience.

Another area in which the boys have participated is membership in after-school clubs. One boy joined the Chess Club and recently played in a Chess Tournament in New York City. Others are members of the American Heritage Club, the Youth Council (a service organization), or the Student Council (student representatives of each class). A class representative was presented with a certificate of service award at the yearly awards assembly. As members of these organizations, they have been able to participate in school sponsored field trips. Some of these one day trips have included visits to Lincoln Center, Broadway shows, museums, libraries, and other cultural places of interest in New York City. In the future, they hope to join groups in longer trips to Albany, New York for visits to the state capitol, to Washington, D.C., and to Philadelphia, Pennsylvania.

Other pupils have joined in after-school sports such as wrestling or gymnastics. Although their participation has hardly been spectacular, they have participated, made friends, and it is hoped the experience has opened the door to new vistas for them and for the instructors who have accepted them.

As members of the regular junior high, these pupils have become involved in community Saturday recreation programs. They have attempted many physical endeavors to which they never would have been exposed otherwise. A few have even attended Friday night recreation and social events and dances.

The point to be remembered is not so much one of evaluating how well they measured up to the other pupils in participating in these activities but rather how many new worlds have been opened providing them with the opportunities to find themselves and where they are best suited to function as worthy, contributing members of society.

This program is still evolving, and we have only begun to scratch the surface of the many areas available where these pupils can possibly participate. One has only to look at the handbook of any junior high school to see the many possibilities. There are clubs, organizations, sports, and many other activities as well as the varied levels offered in academic subjects. If there is any one place that any one of these pupils can function successfully, the regular junior high structure is sure to have it available for them.

We emphasize that the average length of a school day for the typical self-contained brain-injured class is usually shortened to four or five hours, during which they have a lunch and recreation period. This program which originally ran 9 A.M. to 2 P.M. has been successfully lengthened to an almost full day. The pupils can arrive at 8 A.M. for the regular homeroom period and then proceed to follow their schedules according to the same periods of the junior high. Their day can be seven and a half periods in length as compared to the eight periods of the regular school day.

Brain-injured pupils function best when their environment is structured. The regular junior high by its very system of regular time periods offers an excellent structuring device which we have well utilized. This structuring and the fact that the school day is broken up by nonacademic subjects and permissive movements between periods is what we feel makes possible the longer school day. Some pupils are now going the full eight period day and two ninth grade pupils have been integrated into regular homerooms. They follow their individual schedules and come to the special class as a regularly scheduled remedial class.

TABLE 25
PUPIL PROGRAM CARDS*

Student: A Grade: 7   Homeroom: Special Class

Period	Subject	Teacher	Room
1.	Art (grade 7)	Regular Class	#
2.	Remedial Reading (grade 2)	Special Class	#
3.	Arithmetic (grade 4)	Special Class	#
4.	Science and Social Studies	Special Class	#
5.	.... LUNCH		Cafeteria
6.	Spelling and English (grade 2)	Special Class	#
7.	Music (grade 7)—Mon.-Wed.-Fri.	Regular Class	#
	Physical Education (Grade 7)— Tues.-Thur.	Regular Class	Gym
8.	Homeroom and Early Dismissal (2:30 p.m.)	Special Class	#

Speech Improvement—Wednesday 4th period—Speech Teacher

Student: B Grade: 8   Homeroom: Special Class

Period	Subject	Teacher	Room
1.	Art (grade 8)	name	#
2.	Social Studies (grade 7)	name	#
3.	Remedial Reading (grade 4)	Special Class	#
4.	Arithmetic (grade 5)	Special Class	#
5.	.... LUNCH		Cafeteria
6.	Spelling and English (grade 4)	Special Class	#
7.	Music (grade 8)—Mon.-Wed.-Fri.	Special Class	#
	Physical Education (Grade 8)— Tues.-Thur.	Special Class	Gym
8.	Library Council (Library helper)	Special Class	Library

Speech Improvement—Wednesday 4th period—Speech Teacher

---

* Examples taken from actual pupil program cards

TABLE 25 (*Continued*)
PUPIL PROGRAM CARDS*

Student: C *Grade:* 9   *Homeroom:* Regular Ninth Grade Homeroom

Period	*Subject*	*Teacher*	*Room*
1.	Algebra (grade 9)	Regular Class	#
2.	Remedial Reading (grade 7)	Special Class	#
3.	Science (grade 9)	Regular Class	#
4.	Social Studies (grade 9)	Regular Class	#
5.	.... LUNCH		Cafeteria
6.	Industrial Arts (grade 9)	Regular Class	#
7.	English (grade 6) Mon.-Wed.-Fri.	Special Class	#
	Physical Education (grade 9)—	Regular Class	Gym
	Tues.-Thur.		
8.	Spelling (grade 6)	Special Class	#

Speech Correction—Friday 2nd period—Speech Teacher

EXTRA-CURRICULAR ACTIVITIES
Friday night and Saturday recreation programs
Chess Club Member
Student Council Representative
American Heritage Club Member

Student: D *Grade:* 9   *Homeroom:* Regular Ninth Grade

Period	*Subject*	*Teacher*	*Room*
1.	Social Studies (grade 9)	Regular Class	#
2.	Math. (grade 8)	Regular Class	#
3.	Remedial Spelling (grade 6)—	Special Class	#
	Mon.-Wed.-Fri.		
	Physical Education (grade 9)	Regular Class	Gym
4.	General Science (grade 9)	Regular Class	#
5.	.... LUNCH		Cafeteria
6.	Basic Art (grade 9)	Regular Class	#
7.	Remedial Reading (grade 7)	Special Class	#
8.	English (grade 8)	Regular Class	#

EXTRA-CURRICULAR ACTIVITIES
Wrestling Team: 2:45-5:30

---

* Examples taken from actual pupil program cards

DIAGNOSTIC TEACHING

Planning and Providing an Individualized Curriculum

The special class teacher, as can be noted from the previous sections, spends many hours in evaluating the individuals in his class, both formally and informally. Formally, he administers tests to determine grade placement levels in the academic areas. Informally, he observes social and emotional development, behavioral patterns, ability to interrelate with peers and adults, concepts of self, and perceptual development or lack of development.

This information, together with records of past school experiences, is used to formulate a tailor-made program for each pupil. No two students are alike and no two programs can be the same. Each pupil is evaluated individually as to his needs and his strengths. Then an individualized program is drawn up. The student is integrated into regular junior high classes and activities wherever it is indicated he can function successfully. For some, it will be in nonacademic areas only; others may be able, with great effort, to be accepted in only one academic area. Still others are found to be able to tolerate almost a full regular junior high schedule.

In those areas where the pupi is below grade level in academic skills, the special class teacher must develop a remedial program designed to help the pupil overcome his learning disability and thereby improve his academic skills. In some cases this means working with pupils at readiness and preprimer levels as some pupils are illiterate in that they cannot read and have no concept of time, space, letters, or numbers. Other pupils are working at primary levels in one or more areas and at intermediate levels in other areas. Still others can function at junior high levels in many areas but are in need of remedial help or reinforcement in basic language skills.

This, of course, does not make it feasible to have a stationary curriculum for this particular program. The teacher must utilize and draw from the curricula of all levels, depending upon the needs of his group for this particular year, which may not be the same for another year as the group and their needs change.

Since the emphasis of the program stresses getting away from the self-contained atmosphere and stigma as much as possible, the pupils regard their special class teacher as their homeroom teacher and remedial teacher. They come to assigned remedial classes just as they do for any other junior high level class.

Remedial Teaching of the Brain Injured

Diagnostic teaching implies cause and effect of learning disabilities. This is exactly what the teacher must do before she can effectively bring about conceptual learning in the child. If the pupil cannot read for example, the teacher must determine what gap in his perceptual development has been caused by his lesion that makes it difficult or impossible for him to give cognizance to what he hears or sees. If he has not developed laterality or directionality, then he must present the lessons so that laterality and directionality are stressed and developed. If the child has perceptual dysfunctions, then perceptual approaches must be utilized to give meaning to the lesson at hand.

Perceptual training lessons in themselves are not taught so as not to offend the sensitivity of the adolescent who resents and withdraws from what he considers "kid stuff" or "baby books." However, because perceptual training is an integral part of teaching with brain-injured students, perceptual approaches are applied to regular content material. As an example, if a pupil has trouble with staying within an area or in reproducing figures or in cutting a straight line, he would not be asked to color a square, draw a triangle, or cut for the sake of cutting. Instead these same techniques could be applied to more meaningful assignments in social studies or science activities. He could color the areas of a continent, cut out letters or pictures for a bulletin board, or draw simple geometric figures to represent fractions in arithmetic. We have also utilized audiovisual aids such as the opaque projector in making bulletin boards. The pupils trace outlines of related subjects and then paint or color in the objects. This provides perceptual training and also provides a finished product of which the students can be proud to display.

The teacher draws from the perceptual training activities presented in the elementary brain-injured curriculum and adapts them for use to the particular needs of his pupils through content areas at the academic level of the individual. The same technique is used to approach learning situations in all the academic skill areas.

Diagnostic teaching demands that the teacher avoid imposing a curriculum upon the child but rather believes that one be built around the child. The teacher must study the pupil, learn his style of learning, and know that each learning situation is a problem solving one for the pupil. The teacher must evaluate each learning situation in terms of what perceptual skills are involved to accomplish the task and then present the lesson at the level of functioning at which the child is most able to succeed. Multisensory approaches should be injected to each lesson so that the pupil not only sees but also hears and feels concretely the concepts we wish him to form. Temporal sequence is of great importance and each lesson must be presented one small step at a time.

SUMMARY

This view of a program for brain-injured pupils on a junior high level has been presented with the hope that it presents a picture of the *total* involvement of the *total* child in all areas of school *life*. This involvement is intended toward developing an individual who is more ably prepared to face adult life and its demands not only academically but socially and emotionally as well.

Handicaps in themselves are only limiting in the area of the handicap, but handicapping environments such as self-contained classrooms limit every phase of normal development. It is this situation which this program hopes to avoid. It stresses development of the total child in every area and by every means which the regular school situation can offer.

This program is still a growing one and changes yearly to meet the specific needs of the individuals for that year. There were no previous programs as such from which we could draw, and much of the planning has been trial, but so far there has been no real error and much success. No doubt other avenues will avail themselves (as we go along) for us to explore and utilize but the program has now been established through which we can explore and utilize those opportunities for involvement of brain-injured pupils in regular school activities.

PART III
The Severely Physically Handicapped

Chapter 9

A Curriculum for the Severely Crippled Child

Emil Lombardi

INTRODUCTION

CONFLICTS of interest and evaluation have been a constant problem in influencing the developing of programs for multiple
handicapped children. Before we view in detail what should go
into a good curriculum, we must first examine the problems these
children with physical handicaps are forced to face in life from
the time of diagnosis.

One of the major impediments towards sound curriculum development has been a lack of communication between the various
disciplines—the psychologists, the medical men, the occupational
therapists, physiotherapists, teachers, social workers, etc. These
communication difficulties often have stemmed from conflict of
interest partly because of a lack of understanding between the
professionals and their particular contributions and partly because each hopes to have his evaluation and diagnosis given
respect and prominence.

A diagnosis is particularly important with these children. Once
it has been made, whatever the diagnosis may be, the child can
no longer deny the problem or disguise it. (Although, he certainly may try to!) The child must, upon diagnosis, come to grips
with the problem and himself if there is to be any possibility
of growth and remediation. This is important for the professionals
in the field. It is equally important for the parents who have to
work with the children and who are forced to handle the problem.

Too much emphasis has been placed on secondary factors

where the physically handicapped are concerned. Obesity, for example, handicaps many normal people, but the obese child should have every opportunity for advancement in his chosen career. In just such a way we must offer those with physical handicaps, such as being in a wheelchair, every opportunity for growth mentally, socially, and vocationally. We can say then that the wheelchair is a secondary factor not a prime barrier. We want always to go underneath and beyond these cosmetic and physical factors and reach the inner person.

This chapter, then, addresses itself primarily towards developing a structured curriculum for physically handicapped children with the prime focus upon the child as a human being who is a victim of cerebral palsy, or paraplegia, or muscular dystrophy, per se. Educators have long known that each individual varies in his functioning ability. Analysis of such variance with the norm facilitates diagnostic evaluation of an individual's needs. Educators have attempted to implement many variations in curricula in efforts to better educate the multiple handicapped; they speak of "watered down" or "tailor made" curricula. Difficulties in implementing the best course of action in curriculum planning are eased somewhat when the child is normal in intelligence, but even then modifications and enrichments are necessary for the physically handicapped. Certainly no definitive answer to curriculum planning has as yet been determined.

Today, our experiences have guided us into somewhat broader frames of reference with wider resources with which to educate the handicapped child. The physically handicapped need varied experiences as do all children in spite of their handicaps. *Any* experience that will lead to independence physically, mentally, and emotionally must be offered. That is our responsibility and our obligation: to make him as independent an individual as possible. If a child is unable to speak, language development does not cease. We must find a means other than verbal with which such individuals can communicate. If an individual cannot run, we still concern ourselves with resources and ways in which such a person may have an experience in running—maybe by someone running for him or with him—to introduce him to the concept of running. Always we want to at least introduce the child to some proper conceptual framework. Creativity must also be encouraged, be it verbal, artistic, or thought-oriented in nature. Thus, the educator today visualizes a fully integrated program for our handicapped population. In such a program the handicapped child can experience as much as possible the challenges, opportunities, and satisfactions of other children in normal classes. Some children need the combination of special school placement and, where possible, regular school placement to most effectively meet their needs.

REGULAR SCHOOLS

Children with physical handicaps and/or mild problems in the area of motor coordination can easily be integrated into the regular class program if a positive and accepting atmosphere exists on the part of the administration, board of education, and staff. The physical barriers can be thought of as a secondary problem for most of these students, since the various problems of the handicapped can be overcome through trial and error. Should the school offer an educational program for all children of their district with tracks or divisions for slow learners, the mentally retarded, etc., then children with physical disabilities can also be included within the scope of such a program. The factors which would enable physically handicapped children to be integrated into a regular school program would then be evaluated more realistically according to the needs of the child and not on an artificial basis. Too often children are rejected because of insurance liabilities, safety hazards etc. Many schools, were they to be more flexible and compassionate, could bypass these limitations and accept many children who are now rejected.

SPECIAL SCHOOLS

Special schools for the multiple handicapped should take on a flavor of their own in order to provide for the students beyond the needs which may be offered in a regular school. Generally, special schools would feature equipment which would enable the handicapped child to become more independent in his ability to function. Such equipment as hand rails, standing tables, special typewriters, and automatic page-turners would be utilized. Additionally, audio training units, adjustic tables, and specially cut chairs can be used.

A special school should offer the type of supervision, attitudes, and environment which these children need along with the special equipment. When a child needs special services in order for him to be better integrated in his ability to function, a team of educators should evaluate the extent of such needs before placement into a special school is made. Without proper evaluation, some children are limited and become too dependent on the school. Such children, where possible, should be placed in a regular school. It is possible to offer services and attention beyond what a child actually needs. For some balance of evaluation, a team of disciplines utilizing personnel from special settings of both private and public agencies can be helpful. Additionally, personnel from regular schools—administrator, school psychologist, social worker, teachers, and medical doctors—should be used. The combined group would offer not just a superficial evaluation but a total communication which might best fit the child to the extent that it would avoid limiting his growth or at least would let him develop at a faster rate. If one really hopes to offer handicapped children a realistic evaluation for development in the area of formal education, such practice of team approaches would greatly aid in the advancement of suitable programs. The special schools for the handicapped should have close working relations with both private and public agencies and especially with other school districts. Periodiocally, a child may show progress and regressions which need the services and provisions of these agencies in order to make his program more realistic.

A curriculum of subject matter alone can only touch upon one aspect of development for the child with multiple handicaps. Integration with his other needs must be present to offer progress ina meaningful manner. Such services as speech, physiotherapy, occupational therapy, etc. must be offered.

Too often, we make assumptions about why a child is not learning, in fact, the problem is integrative—a disability to use what is being given him in the teaching process, regardless of what we try. The end result is then a variation on a theme: the child can not integrate knowledge being presented.

DIAGNOSTIC TEACHING

Since each child is an individual, and we do give attention to individual needs within ungraded programs with small numbers of students, we can afford variety and a broad range to plan a program that offers more than the regular classroom. A teacher must understand ways to evaluate and put into action the opportunities afforded her in such a setting. Her first responsibility is to know her students well. She should have anecdotal notes along with information at her fingertips which would enable her to best know the children from area to area with assurance and confidence. When the teacher has accomplished this, she will be ready to diagnostically evaluate the gaps that exist within the individuals and plan a program accordingly.

To insure progress in development, one must have guidelines in understanding the individual's needs. One of the many ways to analyze such needs is to ascertain the child's current level of functioning so that we can carefully weigh the assets against the liabilities. From this we could determine the gaps that might be in need of greatest attention. The teacher then would be better able to do diagnostic teaching by realistically attending to the needs of the individual—to himself and to others. With this information, the teacher can offer activities and experiences which will enable the child to truly function at his level of achievement.

Diagnostic teaching calls for examination of curriculum materials on the part of the teacher and ultimate rejection of those which would not be the most beneficial to the development of her students. Curricula should never be a set standard of goals and objectives. A guide for curriculum, particularly with these children, must be flexible and adaptable. In place of a completed, detailed curriculum, I offer on the following pages an aspect of functional sensory training which I consider to be extremely important. It is essentially the basic foundation for building towards the more complex levels of learning with the multiple handicapped. The curriculum on sensory training I offer is necessarily just a suggested one, for the teacher must be flexible in substituting any materials, aids, or resources where he feels it to be applicable. With the multiple handicapped, perhaps more than with any other child, the curriculum depends on past experience, intelligence, and emotional stability.

Objectives of Functional Sensory Training on the Primary Level[4]

I. **Objective 1:** to aid the child in developing positive feelings about his own worth and feelings that the world is a good place in which to live.

  A. To attain this goal we provide:

    1. activities consistent with the child's level of maturation and level of interest so that the factor of sheer competence in handling the material and mastering the activity is in itself self-motivating;

    2. the ratio of child to adult is frequently one-to-one and seldom more than three-to-one so that the child is able to establish a relationship with a concerned and interested adult who accepts him where he is and helps him grow. Honest praise and needed help can be given without delay.

  B. *Techniques and materials used*

    1. Songs and games
       "Touch Your Nose"
       "Where is Lisa's hat?"
       "Two Little Feet"

    2. Riddles
       "My Body"—(learn how to move hands, body, to what extent, etc.)

    3. Finger-plays
       "Eensy Weensy Spider"
       "I'm Very Very Tall"

    4. Use of mirror

    5. Pictures of children and adults of all ethnic groups

    6. Photographs of children taken while child was working at school

    7. Films taken of the children on a trip

    8. Tape recordings—each child has opportunity to recite or sing and tape is made of this performance for the child and class to listen to at various times.

    9. Books—an excellent tool for developing a positive attitude towards oneself

---

[4] Training can start from wherever the child is, regardless of age or level.

Swimming Hole, Two Is a Team, Whistle for Willie, No Bark Dog, A Weed Is A Flower, Empty School House, Galumph, Gilberto and the Wind, Umbrella, Fun for Chris

10. Negro and white dolls, wedgie figures should be part of equipment
11. Resource people (community workers and professionals representative of several racial and ethnic groups)
12. Recognition of birthdays, get-well occasions, and holidays by the sending of individual cards

II. **Objective 2:** to provide consistent, developmental sensory training to enable the child to make use of all five modalities (senses) to receive data for maximum ability in the identification and understanding of himself and his environment.

A. To attain this goal we provide:
 1. a great variety of concrete experiences in the areas of visual, tactual, auditory, olfactory and taste perception;
 2. many materials and games are utilized which involve comparison, discrimination, and differentiation;
 3. where necessary, specific visual perception training along the lines of N. C. Kephart, J. Getman, and M. Frostig is employed.

B. *Techniques and materials used*
 1. Listening games
   "What Instrument is it?"
   "Who is Knocking"—match sound of voice to child
   "Which Bell" (three different size Chinese bells)
   The child descriminates between sounds of bells
   Listen to sounds in room, outdoors, in the school kitchen etc. and identify same
 2. Activity records
   "Sunday in the Park," "Things to Do," "Little Red Bus"
 3. Songs
   Rounds—"Row, Row, Row Your Boat," "Frère Jacques"
   Cumulative songs—"Brought Me A Cat," "Over In the Meadow" Ballads and dialogue—"Gray Goose," "The Fox"
 4. Surprise box
   articles to be identified by touch, such as velvet, feathers, wool, metal, wood, sandpaper, sponge, etc.
 5. Montesorri kits
   color gradation
   texture gradation
   width gradation
   depth gradation

6. Trips
   visits to the bakery, watch a new building being con-
   structed, (feel and see the many types of material);
   many small trips are to be encouraged; seasonal trips
   around the school grounds observing with all the senses
   the many changes.
7. Preparing and eating a variety of simple foods
   (making butter, whipped cream, jello, instant pudding,
   peanut butter and jelly sandwiches, grating carrots)
8. Recognizing food by taste alone
   (salt, sugar, mustard, apples, orange, celery, etc.)
9. Recognizing food and other articles by smell alone
   (cinnamon, apples, orange, soap, cut grass, flowers, paste,
   coffee, maple syrup, fresh bread, etc.)
10. Puzzles
    (valuable in developing visual, motor perception)
    begin with simple one-piece representing entire object
    and gradually add more complicated ones as child develops
    skill.
11. Art
    use of many media for tactual development (sawdust,
    paste, fingerpaint, collages, clay)
12. Games (many varieties)
    lotto
    color cone
    nesting barrels
    postal station
    pegboards and pegs
    checkers
    pick-up sticks

III. **Objective 3:** to train and develop gross and fine muscles and
coordination so as to improve the child's body awareness and to
develop ease in handling materials and the physical ability to use
play materials.

   A. To attain this goal we provide:
      1. opportunities for the child to build a favorable body image;
      2. activities to help the child gain agility in balance and in
         making coordinated movements which will lead to a better
         body schema;
      3. tactile experiences to enable the child to acquire intellectual
         knowledge about his body and its functions so as to increase
         his conscious learning about his body and its relationship
         to his world.

B. *Techniques and materials used*
    1. Rhythm skills
        "I'm Very, Very Tall," "Round and Round the Village,
        To music, respond with body to various rhythms, skipping,
        walking, running, crawling, etc.
    2. Games
        the see-saw, tall and small, reach to the skies, chicken
        wings, tiger hunt, jack-in-the-box, cat and rat.
    3. Physical activity games
        rocking horse; kangaroo hop; dog run; jump and slap;
        elephant walk; walk on a line; log roll; rabbit hop; crab
        walk; jumping jack; rope jumping; bouncing ball; double
        walk; chinese get up; measuring worm; on a line; stunts;
        throwing and catching a ball; hopscotch; alternate toe
        touch; twister; half top spin.
    4. seat work or floor
        modeling clay; hammer and nail sets; Bill Ding Set; Clime
        a Clown; Tinker Toys; Bolt-it Set; Cootie; stringing beads;
        peg-board designs; tracing and cutting; puzzles; parquetry
        blocks; matching designs, shapes and pictures (three di-
        mensional, concrete materials); cutting and pasting; pick-
        up-sticks; building with blocks; sewing; constructing sim-
        ple models.

IV. **Objective 4:** to help the child acquire the skills of expressive and receptive language and an awareness of this tool as an important means of communication.

A. To attain this goal we provide:
    1. a variety of firsthand experiences to serve as stimuli for developing the child's expressive language; animate and in-animate objects are brought into the class sessions to be handled and manipulated; frequent trips are included in this approach;
    2. an abundant supply of carefully screened commercial and originally designed audiovisual materials;
    3. copious use of appropriate books;
    4. activities in finger-plays, games, chants, songs, puppetry, poetry, simple dramatization;
    5. innumerable opportunities for the child to listen to direc-tions, listen for answers, listen to other children in a group, listen to sounds in the school and neighboring streets, listen to records. (All of the above mentioned activities are utilized with related verbalization and/or motor response.)

B. *Techniques and materials used*
1. Three dimensional rubber animals (wild and domestic) family unit, community workers
2. Flannelboard and figures
3. Live pets (rabbit, guinea pig, hamster, white mouse, fish, turtle, frog, salamander, egg hatchery)
4. Live plants (grow potatoe eyes, sweet potato in water, beet and carrot tops, beans, bulbs, seeds, cuttings, force branches of shrubs in early spring)
5. Displays of shells, rocks, leaves, butterflies, insects as motivation for or follow up after a trip to the beach, walk around the school, trip to a park, etc.
6. Dollhouse and furniture
7. Cartons to be turned into a store, stage, post office, ticket office, airport
8. Use of records, tapes, and listening stations, telephones
9. Photographs of children at work in school, going on trips
10. Make album of pictures, display pictures of children on bulletin boards
11. Intercutural approach through use of books and magazines (*Ebony, National Geographic, Nature, Ideal Arizona Highways*)
12. Large, attractive bulletin boards with an intercultural approach through use of pictures
13. Small group activities with an interested adult
14. Care in verbal labeling of articles
15. Combine verbal, visual, and motor approach whenever possible in developing a concept

V. **Objective 5:** to aid the child in developing creative interest in expressing himself through creative media.

A. To attain this goal we provide:
1. direct acquaintance with two and three dimensional materials to enable the child to explore the use of the material (e.g. fingerpaints, tempera colors, collage, wood work, clay, colored chalk, papier mâché, construction paper, fabrics, string straws, pipe cleaners, playdough, etc.);
2. frequent opportunities with the use of art materials to develop concepts of size, and size relationship, shape and form relationship, color and color relationship, space and space relationship, texture, etc.;
3. activities which involve awareness of shape, color, texture in the room and on the child and his companions.

B. *Techniques and materials used*
  1. For the child with limited experiential opportunities, provide a variety of models from which the child may draw. In making a painting of a bird in spring, provide various pictures of birds, their nests, their environment etc. Supply concrete materials such as feathers, straw, thread to be incorporated into the picture.
  2. Accept the child's work of art and make specific comments (e.g. "You have used many bright colors . . . your picture looks very happy"; "I see four circles in your drawing and five very straight lines"; "What shall we call this fine picture, I can count eight colors that you used in drawing your picture, Did I miss any?")
  3. Use music as a means of expressing emotion—happy songs, fast songs, slow music, songs for walking on tip toe—and use of body as a means of responding to music.
  4. Use pantomine, puppetry, and simple dramatization to express oneself in an original story, nursery rhymes, or simple stories (e.g. *Ask Mr. Bear, Caps for Sale, Snowy Day, My Dog is Lost*).

VI. **Objective 6:** to develop the child's awareness of mathematical concepts and their relationship to his world.
  A. To attain this goal we provide:
    1. concrete experiences to establish number names and values;
    2. activities to develop a one-to-one correspondence;
    3. opportunities to deal with geometric shapes;
    4. manipulative activities to establish concept of capacity;
    5. experiences to stack, place, line up etc. a variety of objects so as to develop the number line concept;
    6. concrete experiences to develop understandings of basic mathematical concepts of more or less, in front of and behind, before and after, above and below, first and last.

  B. *Techniques and materials used*
    1. Measuring to follow a recipe—½ lb. butter, 2 eggs
    2. Pouring and measuring water
    3. Measuring wood to make a model
    4. Measuring depth of hole to plant a bulb, seed shrub
    5. Measuring weekly growth of a plant, monthly growth of a child
    6. Matching concrete articles with verbal and visual symbol
    7. Number lotto
    8. Domino
    9. Grouping—more, less, specific amounts

10. Concrete tools—cubes, rods, beads
11. Games "Numerite"
12. Pick-up sticks (certain score for each color)
13. Tossing ball in container (certain score for each size container)
14. Pitching disk on certain areas (specific points for each area)
15. Attention directed to the variation of size and shape in tables, chairs, balls, blocks, windows
16. Blockbuilding as an aid for size and shape relationships
17. One-to-one correspondence (matching pairs—rubbers, mittens)
18. Matching related articles (socks and shoes, plate and spoon)
19. Activities, related to place and direction, space and distance, temperature, weight
20. Experiences in playing store and buying articles

VII. **Objective 7:** to extend the child's horizon by helping him to discover the world of science.

  A. To attain this goal we provide:
   1. opportunities for the child to find satisfaction in questioning, investigating, manipulating, observing, classifying, reporting;
   2. motor-sensory experiences with materials and structures in the school and nearby environment that help the child acquire simple science concepts which aid him in understanding and adjusting to his environment;
   3. a variety of activities for each child to feel that he is a discoverer and that he has something of value to contribute to his group.

  B. *Techniques and materials used*
   1. Care of pets and plants
   2. Birdfeeder at class window
   3. Experiment with water (blowing bubbles, floating objects)
   4. Build and fly a kite
   5. Trips to a beach (classify shells, collect sand, driftwood)
   6. Trips to a bird pond collect feathers
   7. Many opportunities to feel objects, to touch, and to try out
   8. Activities that stimulate observation and comparison
   9. Experiences in making generalization based on concrete situations
   10. Visits to a farm, zoo, woods at different seasons (collect stones, frog eggs, turtle, newt etc.)
   11. Activities pushing and pulling, carrying, etc.

PART IV
Conclusion

Chapter 10

Rounding Out the Curriculum

EDWARD S. STARK

INTRODUCTION

HISTORICALLY, the handicapped child has been somewhat victimized when it came to receiving ancillary services provided normal children. Indeed, the effects of society's victimizing of these children shows a history of exclusions from school, rejections from involvement in normal social interaction, institutionalization, imprisonment, and an attitude effectuated by the society in which he lived of "If we ignore it, maybe we can pretend it doesn't exist."

It would therefore seem quite germaine to include in a book dedicated to exploring curricula for the special child, a chapter dealing with the ancillary services which these children are so often denied. Additionally, previous chapters have tended to stress tool subjects in their curricular considerations. Such ommission does not demonstrate endorsement of a program where these services are ignored.

ANCILLARY SERVICES

Music

In keeping with the history of misconceptions which society has had toward the special child, there were for many years great gaps in their musical education. Prior to the growth of special education and the introduction of the concept of the special teacher, the teaching of music was relegated either to the music teacher or the regular classroom teacher. For many years, neither of these felt competent enough to offer music to the special child.

Additionally, they felt quite uncomfortable in the presence of these children. As a result, music education was lacking. However, with higher level degrees being offered in Special Education, we have seen the birth of a new breed of teacher: the professional, who is competent by virtue of training, emotional stability, and dedication to work directlywith the handicapped whether he be retarded, brain-injured, emotionally disturbed, or physically impaired.

The music program can be taught by the individual classroom teacher as well as by a music specialist. All children in the nursery school and elementary school should have music daily in their own room. With music, disabilities seem to disappear, and self confidence and a feeling of achievement abound. A choral group and even a marching band, are not outside the scope of the possible. Special class students can successfully participate in concert programs as well as in their own classroom programs. The older groups can be taught music theory and can have a program of music appreciation as well.

A well-planned music program can assist in the child's social development, and the child gains through participation in music a feeling of acceptance and success. The child's experiences with rhythm and song are happy and relaxed. The goal of a music program for the special child should be enthusiasm for music. Even the most severely handicapped child can participate, even if the only motion he can make is the tapping of his braces against the wheelchair in accompaniment to the music.

Singing can provide motivation for improvement of expression, comprehension, pronunciation, and respiration. Singing can additionally improve the inflection of the speaking voice and provide better rhythm for speech.

The handicapped child can dance. Even the child in a wheelchair can do interpretive dancing, using those body parts which function. The child in braces can be given dances which are shorter and where less complicated steps have been substituted. The brain-injured child can develop improved sensory motor control through dance and other musical activities, and when properly used, music can even enable the hyperactive brain-injured child to inhibit his random muscular impulses. Awkward movements can turn into graceful ones through the media of the dance.

Many of the children can learn to play a musical instrument. (Yes, even the brain-injured.) Even the child with severe athetoid cerebral palsy can play a xylophone, wrist bells, or hand bells. Two handicapped children could even play duets by telephone if they were confined to home by inclement weather or illness.

Home Economics

Too many times, children in special education are denied opportunities to share in home economics courses. For the special classes, home economics should be offered to boys as well as girls, since the program should include a course in everyday living in addition to regular homemaking. Children who become self-sufficient in everyday living feel self-confidence and pride. They develop initiative and independence. The special child is taught habits of personal cleanliness, making beds, doing laundry and dishes, cooking, sewing, child care, home management, and meal planning.

The home economics room ideally should contain two kitchens, one regular kitchen and one specially adapted to the needs of the severely physically handicapped. However it is important for the crippled child to learn to work effectively in a normal kitchen, since it is unlikely that he will have the benefit of an adapted kitchen in his own home.

Library Services

Ideally, the librarian should be a special education library teacher, with training in both library science and special education, and the library should be a fully equipped resource room. The library program is similar to the program found in regular schools with a few exceptions.

There is a need for a wide assortment of high interest, low level books, for those children who are retarded readers. Stories about handicapped people are chosen with discretion, as handicapped children prefer to read about able-bodied people. Some biographies of handicapped people may be selected such as those of Helen Keller and Franklin Delano Roosevelt.

Where it is feasible, the children are taught all the basic library skills; the use of the catalog, care of books, and research skills. The younger children enjoy the library story hour, while the older groups become involved in animated discussion.

The library should offer a wealth of information in the area of community services for the handicapped, travel opportunities for the disabled, occupational and vocational possiblities, recreational facilities and special programs, institutions of higher learning which have been adapted for use by the physically crippled, etc.

The special librarian or the regular librarian who deals with special children should be constantly searching for good books in the fields of psychological and sexual characteristics of the handicapped adolescent to supplement instruction in sex education and teen age hygiene.

Particular attention must be given to the reference collection, since many of the students are unable to use the public library. Special children often develop a great love of reading, as it is a sedentary activity which can be enjoyed even by the homebound.

Art

The art program can be carried out by the individual classroom teacher as well as a consultant art teacher. The curriculum is usually not a modified one, and the youngsters can work in every possible media. The high school students can also learn the basic elements of good design and layout.

Museum visits can be arranged as often as possible, and to supplement this, programs have been successfully initiated whereby an artist-of-the-month show, representing professional art talent, is displayed. Prominent painters and sculptors are invited to visit the school, at which time they speak to the children and, where possible, demonstrate their work. Samples of their completed work are studied and then are loaned to the school where they are placed on exhibit for a month. The school should strive to have a permanent collection of art works for display both indoors and outdoors.

Occasionally, in art, some aid must be given to the crippled child, such as taping the paper to the table to prevent slipping or providing a lapboard to work on. Devices and gadgetry are used only when absolutely necessary.

Art concepts can be more successfully introduced into the curriculum for the retarded then has heretofore been established. The retarded child can manipulate art media, enjoy color blendings, and, indeed, can enjoy abstract art much more so than had been assumed in the past. He can even contribute his work to art displays; indeed his interest in art can be correlated with occupational or recreational skills. In art, as in music, the handicapped child can function in many ways like the normal child. It is one more area in which the special child can develop self-confidence and a genuine feeling of accomplishment.

Physical Education

Every child is entitled to participate in a physical education program, for even children with severe degrees of physical impairment crave physical activity.

An adapted or modified program for the special child would:

1. be an individualized program designed to meet the specific needs of each child;
2. encourage group activities to foster improved social and emotional adjustments;
3. aid in the development of healthy and intelligent attitudes toward the particular handicap;
4. improve or remediate deviations in posture and body mechanics.

Some modifications that can be made in the physical education program include: the use of substitute runners (if one is in a wheelchair); a decrease in the number of repetitions; restrictions in amount of time to be "It" in a game; simplification of rhythms or steps in a dance; etc. It is always important to strive to play all games as close to the official rules as is possible.

The physical education teacher for the special classes must

have complete medical information and doctor's advice and permission before beginning a program for a special child. In dealing with the brain-injured child, he should consult with the psychologist or classroom teacher for additional information on perceptual deficits. With the emotionally disturbed youngster, information should be available from the psychologist to aid in planning a suitable physical education experience.

The physical education program for special children may include all sports: hockey, baseball, basketball, soccer, shuffleboard, ping-pong, volleyball, archery, badminton, golf, games, dances, and even bowling. (If the school is not equipped to offer such a broad range of activities it is suggested that the school use community facilities.) Special class children have even become so competent in sports as to be included on intramural and intermural sports.

When the building contains a swimming pool, swimming should be included in the program for the special children, for it is both enjoyable and therapeutic. A physical therapist can be a consultant to the school to work with the children in the swimming program and in the gymnasium. A complete gymnasium, which considers the full range of special handicaps, should include stairways, bar bells, pulleys, weights, exercycles, chinning equipment, and other facilities for physical therapy and general physical fitness actitivies.

The classroom teacher can use physical education in her daily program by having finger limbering exercises before writing, deep breathing exercises before singing; by having children take action poses as models for painting, drawing, or clay work; and by having children use large muscles in cleaning the blackboards or tables.

In the public schools, the children in the special education program can participate in the regular physical education curricula on an integrated basis with only minimal adjustments. The children in the special classes profit from being integrated into the regular physical education classes as early as possible.

PREPARING FOR THE WORLD OF WORK

On the secondary level, a program for the handicapped child should offer a business or pre-vocational course as well as an academic course. It should include a complete business program with courses in typing, use of business machines, simple accounting, business math, business law and theory, and computer techniques.

The emphasis in vocational guidance should be upon exposure. The handicapped child needs to gain a thorough knowledge of the world of work. It is important to visit places of employment as well as to invite career speakers, both handicapped and non-handicapped. The child must learn what the physical and mental requirements are in the various occupations in order to make a wise choice.

Vocational guidance is a team effort. Cooperation must be forthcoming from the community at large through a program of community education in the area of the special child. Much of the work is coordinated by the school guidance counselor with help available from agencies such as the Division of Vocational Rehabilitation.

In New York City, in their health conservation classes, vocational training is started early, with all the children participating in an exploratory shop cycle. In California, programs have been successfully developed wherein special children are provided with actual job work experience, which leads to more realistic vocational goals.

The vocational teacher of the special child must endeavor to teach self-reliance, initiative, self-esteem, and reassurance, and he should gain great satisfaction from giving the students a feeling of self-confidence as well as having them learn to do their jobs well.

Index